T

TECHNICAL ANALYSIS

MASTERCLASS

- Master The Financial Markets –

Rolf Schlotmann & Moritz Czubatinski

Company identity
Quantum Trade Solutions GmbH
Jahnstrasse 43
63075 Offenbach
Germany

Chairmen: Schlotmann, Rolf and Czubatinski, Moritz

Publication date: 19.02.2019
1st print

ISBN: 9781795471855
Imprint: Independently published

Financial charts have been obtained through www.tradingview.com

Foreword

Introduction

Foreword

I am so happy to see Rolf writing a trading book. I have enjoyed watching him share some of the best educational material for new traders online, and I have been continually impressed with the work he's done on his trading journal, EdgeWonk. His thorough understanding of price action trading, 15 years of experience and attention to detail are all evident in his work. While you can learn a lot about the markets by studying his infographics online, this book takes it a step further by explaining the timeless principles of technical analysis that measure the emotions and trends of the market. It illustrates how to trade price action and demystifies chart patterns with a common sense approach. It's important to realize that there's more to trading than memorizing patterns. It's critical that traders learn to manage their risk and their emotions for long term success, and Rolf does a great job of sharing these principles and making them applicable to technical chart analysis in all financial markets. Rolf set out to write the trading book he wished he had when he started his trading journey 15 years ago, and in the process, he created the book that every new trader will be thankful for.

Steve Burns

NewTraderU.com

Introduction

Trading stocks, currencies, futures, options and other financial contracts is not actually complicated and anybody can learn it in a relatively short time. This has been my daily experience for the past decade and even traders who have tried everything for years without success can potentially make their first profits if the art of trading is explained to them in the right way. However, the keyword "in the **right** way" is important here.

I was first introduced to trading 15 years ago and it took me several years to acquire a solid trading knowledge. Looking back, I can say that I have spent too much time and money on my training and most of it was simply wrong. Of course, as a newbie, you cannot judge that. In only a few weeks, I can now teach new traders the things for which I needed up to five years in the early days of my trading. By now, more than 1000 traders have already gone through my online trading training and I would now like to pass on the experience which I have gained through my own trading and the daily work with traders, in this book.

On the one hand, I would like to make it easier for new traders to enter the world of financial markets and technical analysis and, on the other hand, I want to show experienced traders a more effective approach to chart reading so that those will also benefit from the trading strategies and tips outlined in this book.

This book focuses on technical analysis, explanation and interpretation of price movements and chart patterns as well as on learning effective, ready-to-use trading strategies. However, it is important to go beyond the usual technical analysis, and to analyse the behaviour of traders based on psychological factors and phenomena of mass psychology as well.

The price movements on the international financial markets arise because millions of people interact with each other every day. Buying and selling decisions are influenced by emotions and human behavioural patterns. Whether we are looking at a speculator from China 200 years ago, a Wall Street pit trader from New York 80 years ago or a modern-day "Joe Bloggs trader", trading from his/her smartphone – the human components, i.e. emotions and instincts, hardly differ. Greed, fear, uncertainty and the willingness to take risks have determined human actions for millennia and, of course, also how people have manoeuvred their money around the world's markets for decades. Those who learn to read the buyer and seller interaction from the charts will be able to read and handle any price movement, on any financial market and on all time frames. This is true because all price charts follow universal and timeless rules that can be successfully interpreted with the help of effective technical analysis.

Most trading books and websites recommend that traders memorise certain price patterns and formations and call this technical analysis. But such an approach only promotes stereotyped thinking which, however, is not expedient and can even have negative consequences. The financial markets are dynamic and no two price movements are identical. Memorisation limits the trader only to the patterns they have learnt. What a trader really needs instead is a step-by-step education that enables him/her to interpret and correctly classify every possible scenario.

Over the years, more than one million visitors have already searched for information about trading on our website www.tradeciety.com. Every day, traders ask us how they can understand technical analysis and price movements in a better manner. This book is a result of the motivation to answer these questions collectively. It is the book I would have wished for at the beginning of my trading career over 15 years ago.

The first section of this book provides comprehensive knowledge of the fundamentals and individual components of technical analysis and price analysis. The second section focuses on the most important chart patterns as well as the correct interpretation of chart formations. We will explore potential entry signal points and trading strategies so that traders can now already make sense of their own charts with confidence. In addition to an insight into important psychological trading concepts, traders will get numerous practical tips to ensure that they handle their trading professionally at the end of this book.

The goal of this book is it to enable the reader to look behind the price movements and understand **why** prices rise and fall, how buyers and sellers interact and thus to make effective trading decisions. The comprehensive and step-by-step approach of mastering technical analysis ultimately makes it possible to interpret any chart situation and, thus, hopefully become an independent trader.

1. What is trading?

To understand our role as traders better, we need to ask ourselves – what is trading really about?

The commonly used definition of trading is: a trader tries to **make a profit** by entering into trades or **betting on price movements**, by anticipating the **future price trend** as correctly as possible.

We will now examine the various components of this definition in more detail.

1.1 The profit potential

In trading, it is possible to bet on **rising** as well as on **falling** prices and thus to make a profit even if the stock market or another financial market falls.

If the trader believes, based on the findings of his/her analysis, that the stock of Apple ® or the exchange rate between the EUR and the USD will appreciate, he/she can buy the shares or the corresponding currencies today and sell them at a higher price later to make a profit.

And even if the trader assumes that prices will go down, he/she can take this into account in his/her trading plan and enter a so-called sell (short) trade with which he/she profits when prices on the underlying assets depreciate.

Naturally there is always the risk that the price trend will not be as per the trader's expectations and hence he/she has to close the trade with a loss.

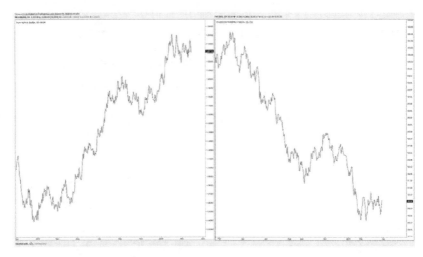

Figure 1: Left: EUR-USD chart. A trader can make profits by betting on rising rates when the exchange rate rises. Right: USD exchange rate. If a trader enters a sell trade at a right time, he/she can make profits when the rate drops.

1.2 Decision-making

To make buying or selling decisions, traders can use various methods and tools to analyse price movements in the price charts and stock prices.

A distinction is made between the **fundamental data trader**, who makes trading decisions based on company or economic data, and the so-called **technical trader**, who only analyses share prices and focuses on specific patterns and price formations.

It is difficult to generalise that a particular type of decision-making or analysis is superior to the other. Rather, it is important that the individual trader chooses the type of trading that suits him/her better. This book exclusively focuses on understanding and applying the concepts of technical analysis.

1.3 Short-term vs. long-term trading

The investment horizon is an important topic that fundamentally determines the type of trading. We normally distinguish between two groups: **day trading** and **swing trading**.

In case of short-term trading, the trader opens and closes his/her individual trades within a few minutes or hours. Since the speculative period is usually limited to one day, these trades are called **day trading**.

If the holding period of a position is a few days to weeks or even months, it is called **swing trading**.

The application possibilities of these two trading types and the respective requirements for traders are fundamentally different.

Day trading is often less suitable for employed people due to time constraints, since it is often necessary to keep an eye on price charts throughout the opening hours of the market. When the Frankfurt Stock Exchange opens at 9.00 AM, most people in Germany are probably at work and cannot follow the price movements actively. However, a German day trader could alternatively switch to other stock markets and actively trade on the American or Asian stock exchanges after his/her working hours.

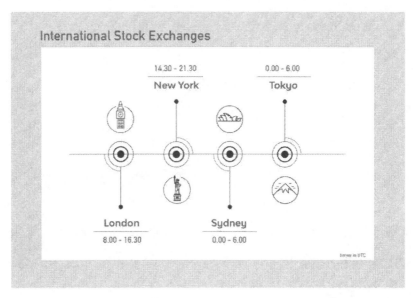

Figure 2: Daily opening times of the most important international finance markets. Timey may change during DST.

Most people find it far more practical to limit themselves to medium to longer-term swing trading since the time involvement can be considerably less. Swing trading is often the better solution for employed people, since they don't have to sit in front of a PC for hours and the decision-making process is slower.

2. What is technical analysis?

Technical analysis is a concept that can be used to analyse the price movements of financial instruments with the objective of identifying profit opportunities.

The benefits of technical analysis have been often discussed but it is also important to look at the criticism of this concept at this point to understand all the implications.

Scientists, and especially the proponents of the efficient market hypothesis, compare technical analysis with pure speculation, whereby a reference to the popular dart-throwing monkey experiment is often made[1].

On the other hand, a report by Neely and Weller confirms that technical analysis might be superior to fundamental data analysis in the short-term investment horizon[2]. Y. Zhu and G. Zhou recognise that the momentum effect can be a potentially profitable technical strategy based on historical price patterns[3]. A study of over 2,000 Chinese stocks confirmed that the effectiveness of the analysis could be significantly improved with

---

[1] *Arnott R., Hsu J, Kalesnik V, Tindall P (2011): "The Surprising Alpha from Malkiel's Monkey and Upside-Down Strategies". The Jounral of Portfolio Management. Volume 39, Number 4. 2013.*

[2] Neely C. and Weller P.: "Technical Analysis in the Foreign Exchange Market". Federal Reserve Bank of St. Louis.

[3] Zhu Y., Zhou G. (2009): "Technical Analysis: An asset allocation perspective on the use of moving averages". Journal of Financial Economics 92.

the support of technical tools[4]. Another study of the Russian stock market suggests that trading systems that use technical indicators might outperform a simple "buy-and-hold" strategy[5].

2.1 Technical analysis and crowd psychology

Prices on the financial markets move, among other things, because millions of people and institutions interact on the international financial markets every day. Financial market players make buying and selling decisions that influence the pricing of financial instruments and cause upward and downward prices fluctuations.

Technical analysis is so effective because people always follow the same behavioural patterns and often make their trading decisions collectively based on similar emotions.

Most people will already know sayings like "greed is good" or "shares are bought based on expectations and not based on facts". This indicates that the human psyche and general thinking patterns are an important part of developments on the financial markets. Whether we are looking at a speculator from China 200 years ago, a Wall Street pit trader from New York 80 years ago or

---

[4] Li G. and Zhu J. (2014): "Research on the Effectiveness of Technical Indicators with the Volume". International Conference on Education, Management and Computing Technology.
[5] Chsherbakov V.: "Efficiency of Use of Technical Analysis: Evidences from Russian Stock Market".

a modern-day "Joe Bloggs Trader" – the human components, i.e. emotions and instincts, hardly differ. Greed, fear, uncertainty and the willingness to take risks have determined human actions for millennia and, of course, how people have manoeuvred their money around the world's markets for centuries. When we learn to read the buyer and seller interaction from the charts, we will be able to read and handle any price chart, on any market and for all times going forward.

Another important reason why technical analysis is so effective is because of the principle of the **self-fulfilling prophecy.** Since millions of people follow the concepts of technical analysis and make decisions based on them, they verify the fact that technical indicators and other concepts work simply because they are widespread. Even the financial media often refer to technical concepts such as past highs and lows, all-time highs and lows, psychologically important price levels and moving averages.

When we delve into the analysis of pricing structures and chart studies during this book, you will soon realise that technical trading is much more than it seems at first glance. We will develop an understanding that will enable us to put ourselves in the shoes of other traders and interpret the thought processes of financial market players, so that we can ultimately benefit from technical analysis through independent strategic thinking.

Most traders carry out technical analysis only at an extremely superficial level since the majority of the literature does not usually deal with the underlying mechanisms in-depth. Here, the criticism by the opponents of technical analysis would even be justified, because such an approach is not effective and trading cannot be reduced to surface level thinking. This book has the goal to explore technical analysis in a new and more effective way.

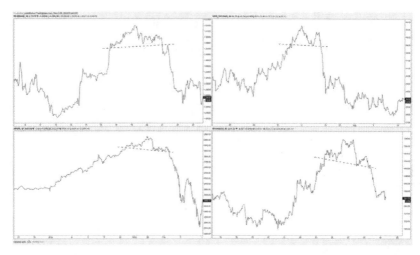

Figure 3: Whether we follow the USD-CAD currency pair, the Porsche® share price, the S&P 500 or gold, the same patterns are observable everywhere which indicates the importance of technical analysis. Principles of technical analysis are timeless.

3. Introduction to candlestick analysis

We will start with the fundamentals of technical analysis and then progress step by step to the advanced concepts so that, at the end of this book, we will be able to interpret and trade with any kind of chart.

Even those who have prior experience in trading should not skip the following section. It contains a different approach that is not often addressed in conventional technical analysis and it is a prerequisite for a successful price analysis.

3.1 Line charts

For most people, line charts usually provide the first impression of the world of financial markets because we see them frequently when we open the newspaper or turn on the television.

A line chart can describe the price development of a stock, a currency pair, a cryptocurrency, a commodity and any other financial value. The advantage of a line chart is that the information is highly compressed. One glance at the line chart tells you all that you want to know for a first elementary analysis.

If we see a rising line chart, it indicates a rally or a **bull market** (a bull thrusts its horns in the air). If the line chart shows a falling price, it indicates a **bear market** (the bear swipes his paws down).

The closing prices for a day are usually plotted and joined together in a line chart. Every day, we move one time unit to the right on the scale. This kind of chart is also called a **daily chart**.

The disadvantage of a line chart is that the price fluctuations **within** a day – or any chosen time period - cannot be recorded since the line chart shows only the closing prices. However, we all know that there can be strong price fluctuations in the financial markets and neglecting them can be a disadvantage for the precise technical analysis.

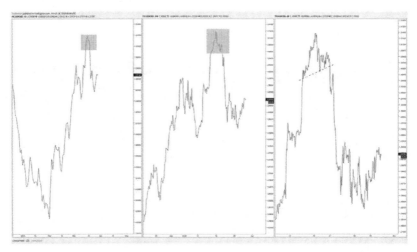

Figure 4: The market snapshot shows the USD and CAD exchange rate. *The **day** period is selected on the left, the **4-hour** period in the middle and the **1-hour** period on the right. The deeper we go in the chart periods, the more details we can see.*

3.2 Candlestick charts

Candlestick charts are further developed line charts that serve to compensate for the disadvantage of less information. Candlestick charts have their origin in 17th century Japan. Today, candlestick charts are the preferred tool of analysis for traders and most investors since they provide all the required information at a glance.

3.2.1 The candlestick

As the name suggests, a candlestick chart is made up of so-called (price) **candlesticks**. These candlesticks are made up of different components to describe the price movements of financial instruments.

Two sample candlesticks are shown in figure 5. A candlestick consists of a solid part, the **body**, and two thinner lines which are called **candle wicks** or **candlestick shadows**.

The candlesticks are **color-coded** to illustrate the direction of the price movements. A white candlestick represents rising prices, whereas a black candlestick shows that the price fell during the period.

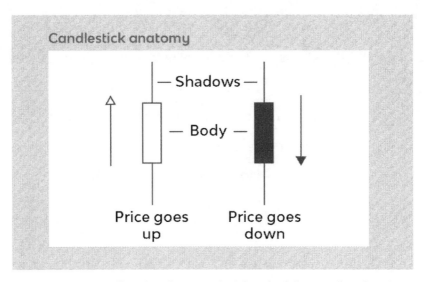

Figure 5: A rising candlestick is shown on the left and a falling candlestick is shown on the right along with the explanations of terms used for individual candlestick components.

The length of the **shadows** shows how much the price has moved up and down with respect to a candlestick within a specific duration. If we set our charts so that one candlestick corresponds to one day, then we can read the daily fluctuations in the financial market using the shadows of a candlestick.

The **candlestick body** describes the difference between the opening and closing prices for the corresponding time period.

The body of the white, rising candlestick in figure 6 shows that the price opened at $10 and closed at $20 in the selected time interval, but has fluctuated between $25 and $5 in the meantime, as indicated by the shadows.

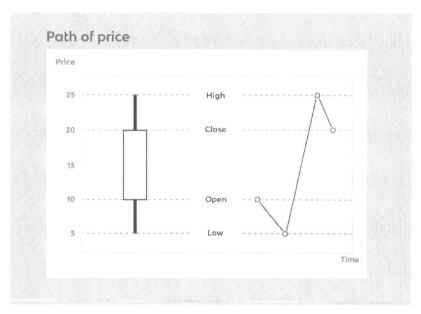

Figure 6: The trend of candlesticks from the opening price to the closing price is described by the candlestick body. The shadows show the entire fluctuation width.

If we line up several candlesticks, we can reproduce the progression of line charts by following the candlestick bodies as shown in figure 7. The candle shadows also show the severity of price fluctuations in each case. We, thus, get all the information that is essential for an effective price analysis at a glance. This is why candlestick charts are mostly used for technical analysis these days.

17

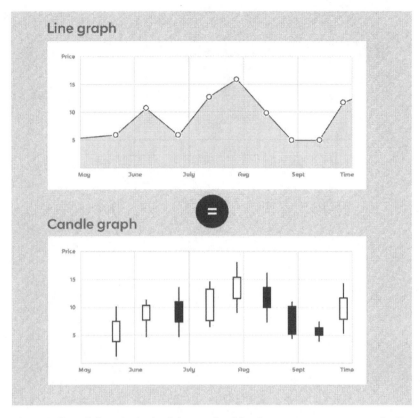

Figure 7: If you follow the path of the candlestick prices, you can reconstruct the line charts. Candlesticks offer more information and are the preferred medium for technical analysts.

The following chapters show how to interpret this information usefully to make actual trading decisions. Anyone who knows how to analyse and interpret the so-called candlestick patterns or candle formations, already understands the actions of the financial market players a little better.

3.3 Basics of candlesticks

Candlesticks can be divided into four elements, where each element reveals a different aspect of the current trading behaviour and the prevailing market sentiment.

3.3.1 Intro: The strength ratio – bulls vs. bears

To understand the price and candlestick analysis, it helps if you imagine the price movements in financial markets as a battle between the buyers and the sellers. Buyers speculate that prices will increase and drive the price up through their trades and/or their buying interest. Sellers bet on falling prices and push the price down with their selling interest.

If one side is stronger than the other, the financial markets will see the following trends emerging:

- If there are more buyers than sellers, or more buying interest than selling interest, the buyers do not have anyone they can buy from. The prices then increase until the price becomes so high that the sellers once again find it attractive to get involved. At the same time, the price is eventually too high for the buyers to keep buying.
- However, if there are more sellers than buyers, prices will fall until a balance is restored and more buyers enter the market.

- The greater the imbalance between these two market players, the faster the movement of the market in one direction. However, if there is only a slight overhang, prices tend to change more slowly.
- When the buying and selling interests are in equilibrium, there is no reason for the price to change. Both parties are satisfied with the current price and there is a market balance.

It is always important to keep this in mind because any price analysis aims at comparing the strength ratio of the two sides to evaluate which market players are stronger and in which direction the price is, therefore, more likely to move.

3.3.2 Element 1: Size of the candlestick body

The size of the candlestick body shows the difference between the opening and closing price and it tells us a lot about the strength of buyers or sellers.

Below, the most important characteristics of the analysis of the candlestick body are listed.

- A **long candlestick body,** that leads to quickly rising prices, indicates more buying interest and a strong price move.

- If the size of the candlestick bodies **increases** over a period, then the price trend **accelerates** and a trend is intensified.

- When the size of the bodies **shrinks**, this can mean that a prevailing trend comes to an end, owing to an increasingly balanced strength ratio between the buyers and the sellers.

- Candlestick bodies that **remain constant** confirm a stable trend.

- If the market **suddenly** shifts from long rising candlesticks to long falling candlesticks, it indicates a sudden change in trend and highlights strong market forces.

Figure 8: Left: Long candlestick bodies during the downward and upward trend phases. Sideways phases are usually characterized by smaller bodies. Right: Rising

candlesticks are stronger in the upward trend. At the peak, the ratio tilts and a sideways phase is characterized by smaller candlesticks.

3.3.3 Element 2: Length of candlestick shadows

The length of shadows helps in determining the volatility, i.e. the entire range of price fluctuations.

Characteristics of candlestick-shadow analysis:

- Long shadows can be a sign of **uncertainty** because it means that the buyers and sellers are strongly competing, but neither side has been able to gain the upper hand so far.

- Short shadows indicate a **stable** market with little instability.

- We can often see that the length of the candlestick shadows **increases** after long trend phases. Increasing fluctuation indicates that the battle between buyers and sellers is intensifying and the strength ratio is no longer as one-sided as it was during the trend.

- **Healthy** trends, which move quickly in one direction, usually show candlesticks with only small shadows since one side of the market players dominates the proceedings.

3.3.4 Element 3: Body to shadow ratio

For a better understanding of price movements and market behaviour, the first two elements must be correlated in the third element.

Important factors in this context are:

- During a **strong trend**, the candlestick bodies are often significantly longer than the shadows. The stronger the trend, the faster the price pushes in the trend direction. During a strong upward trend, the candlesticks usually close near the high of the candlestick body and, thus, do not leave a candlestick shadow or have only a small shadow.

- When the **trend slows down**, the ratio changes and the shadows become longer in comparison to the candlestick bodies.

- **Sideways phases** and **turning points** are usually characterised by candlesticks that have a long shadow and only short bodies. This means that there is a relative balance between the buyers and the sellers and there is uncertainty about the direction of the next price movement.

Figure 9: There are almost no shadows during the left rising phase, confirming the strong trend. Suddenly long candlestick shadows are visible in the sideways phase; these indicate uncertainty and an intensified battle between the buyers and the sellers. When candlestick shadows increase, it can foreshadow the end of a trend.

3.3.5 Element 4: Position of the body

As far as the position of the candlestick body is concerned, we can distinguish between two scenarios in most cases:

- If you see only one dominant shadow which sticks out on one side and the candlestick body is on the opposite side, then this scenario is referred to as **rejection**, a

24

hammer or a **pinbar**. The third and the seventh example in figure 10 show such candlesticks. The shadow indicates that although the price has tried to move in a certain direction, the opposition of market players has strongly pushed the price in the other direction. This is an important behaviour pattern which we will analyse in detail later.

- Another typical scenario shows a candlestick with two equally long shadows on both sides and a relatively small body. The fifth candlestick in figure 10 shows such an **indecision** candlestick. On one hand, this pattern can indicate uncertainty, but it can also highlight a balance between the market players. The buyers have tried to move the price up, while the sellers have pushed the price down. However, the price has ultimately returned to the starting point.

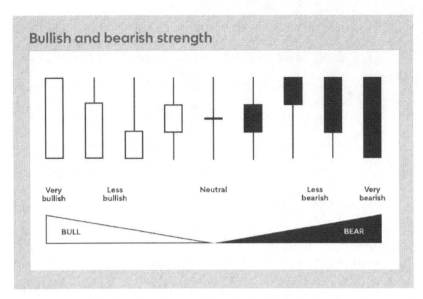

Figure 10: From left to right: The size of the candlestick body describes the strength of the price movement. The longer the body, the stronger the impulse. If the candlestick shadows are longer, there is a balance between the sellers and the buyers and the indecision increases.

3.4 Mastering candlestick patterns

If you open any trading book about candlestick analysis or do a Google search for candlestick patterns, you will immediately get dozens of different patterns. Conventional technical analysis suggests that a trader should learn all these different patterns and respective meanings to spot them on the price charts during actual trading.

In my opinion, mindless memorisation is not required and it is also not effective since all candlesticks can consist of only the four aforementioned elements. Another risk of pure memorisation is that a trader loses the big picture. **Template-thinking** should be avoided in trading. Once a trader understands how to interpret the price information in the right context, he/she can immediately understand and trade with any price chart. In addition, the trader is not only restricted to the candlestick patterns learned, but can interpret and correctly classify every possible scenario.

In the technical analysis, we normally differentiate between single candle and multiple candle patterns. As the name suggests, in the **single candlestick analysis** only a single candlestick is examined for specific characteristics to interpret the prevailing market mood. In the **multiple candlestick analysis,** up to three consecutive candlesticks are analysed. The most important patterns and the options for their interpretation are illustrated in the next chapter using the four elements from the previous section. The goal is to discard template-thinking to be able to anticipate each scenario correctly.

3.5 The most important single candle patterns

3.5.1 Pinbar

The pinbar is probably the most well-known candlestick pattern. A pinbar has only one long shadow, which sticks out to one side. The body of a pinbar is at the opposite end of the shadow. It is not so important whether the candlestick has a large or small body as long as price does not leave a second shadow.

A pinbar after a long uptrend often signifies an imminent **sell-off.** It is, therefore, also listed under the trend reversal candlesticks because it indicates that an existing trend is coming to an end. If you see a pinbar with a long upstanding shadow, like in figure 11, in an upward trend, it means that although the buyers have tried to push the price up, the interest to sell has suddenly increased and the sellers have reversed the price direction. The body of a candlestick like this should therefore close at the lower end to signal that the sellers have pushed the price below the opening price and the reverse signal has thus been strengthened downwards.

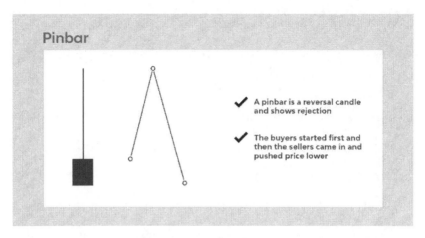

Figure 11: The elements of a pinbar candlestick include a long shadow and one comparatively smaller body. The pinbar shows a price reversal and/or a rejection. After an uptrend, such a pinbar could foreshadow a potential downward trend.

3.5.2 The Hanging Man

The Hanging Man is also one of the trend reversal candlesticks, but it differs from the Pinbar as far as the characteristics and interpretation are concerned.

In an upward trend, a candlestick with a long downward shadow, like in figure 12, means that interest in selling has suddenly increased and sellers have managed to move the price down sharply. This should prick up buyers' ears, because the price usually moves upwards in a straight line during a healthy upward trend since buying interest absorbs all sellers. The body of the Hanging Man is often relatively small and there is little difference between the opening and closing prices. The Hanging Man can have a small second shadow, which is usually not pronounced. Its main feature is the long shadow against the prevailing trend direction, which shows the newly developed interest of the opposition.

If the buyers withdraw completely, the price can often easily start a new downward trend, because the Hanging Man has already indicated that the sellers have taken their positions.

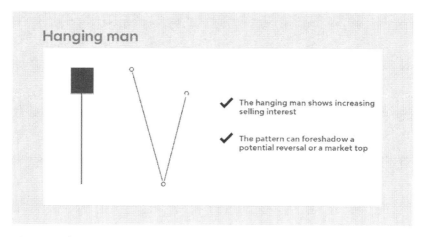

Figure 12: The Hanging Man indicates that the strength ratio moves slowly. After an uptrend phase, the downward shadow confirms that more sellers are entering the market.

3.5.3 Marubozu

The interpretation of the Marubozu candlestick is clear because the Marubozu candle consists only of a long candlestick body without any shadows. The Marubozu candlestick is also known as an impulse, momentum or trend continuation candlestick because it indicates that the candle has only moved in one direction from the opening time to the closing time. The longer the Marubozu candlestick is, compared to the previous candlesticks, the stronger the trend signal. A trader can then expect the prevailing trend to continue. During an upward trend, the Marubozu candlestick shows that there is no selling interest and that the buyers can easily drive the price up.

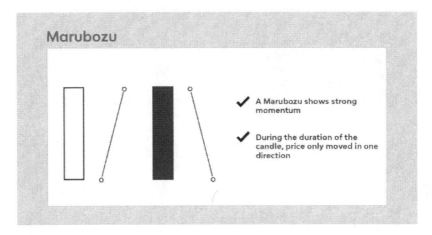

Figure 13: The Marubozu candlestick consists only of a candlestick body and is a strong impulse candle.

3.5.4 The Doji

The Doji is a well-known candlestick pattern, but with a little informative value on its own. The Doji is a neutral candlestick, which consists of two shadows of equal length and only a small body. The two shadows indicate that the buyers as well as the sellers have tried to steer the price in a particular direction, but there was no overweight and the price has eventually returned to the opening price. The Doji thus indicates a temporary pause and indecision by the market players.

If a Doji occurs during a trend phase, it usually has no significance and everything depends on the candlestick that follows as we will see in the following multi-candlestick analysis section.

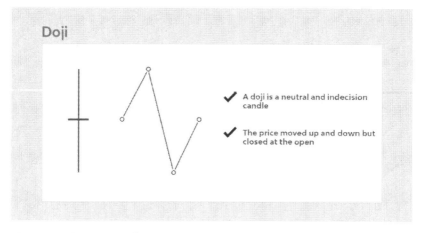

Figure 14: The Doji candlestick indicates a temporary pause and the equilibrium between the buyers and the sellers.

3.6 Multiple candles pattern

Multiple candles patterns are based on the aforementioned four candlestick elements and they are also made of the described single candles from the previous pages. We simply need to follow the **price path** and then analyse it in the context that we have learnt until now.

Multiple candles patterns have a greater predictive power than single candles, because the simultaneous analysis of multiple candles can make use of double or triple information content. Caginalp and Laurent have shown in their research that certain multiple candles patterns, such as the Three White Soldiers or the Three Black Crows, might have significant short-term predictive power. They confirmed that these patterns could enable correct predictions of up to 75%. [6]

The most well-known multiple candles patterns are presented in this chapter.

---

[6] G. CAGINALP and H. LAURENT: The predictive power of price patterns (1998), Applied Mathematical Finance 5, 181–205

3.6.1 The Engulfing candlestick

The Engulfing formation consists of two successive candlesticks, wherein the second candlestick is significantly larger than the first and engulfs it completely.

The second candlestick often resembles the Marubozu candlestick, which consists only of a long body without a shadow.

If the candlesticks initially become smaller during a downward trend, they indicate that the sellers are slowly withdrawing from the market. The following engulfing candlestick then signals that the strength ratio suddenly reverses and more buyers enter the market so rapidly that they explosively reverse the trend direction within a single candlestick. In this context, the Engulfing formation is a reversal signal: the price then has a higher probability of moving further in the direction of the Engulfing candlestick since the strength ratio has shifted on one side.

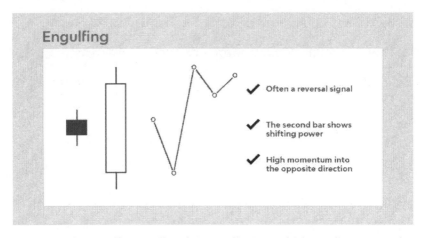

Figure 15: The Engulfing candlestick is an effective multiple candles pattern that describes the sudden and strong change in direction.

3.6.2 Three Black Crows (3BC)/Three White Soldiers (3WS)

The 3BC formation is a signal for the trend continuation. It shows how the sellers are pushing buyers out of the market. Figure 16 shows that the 3BC formation consists of three consecutive downwards candlesticks, where each candle starts at a higher opening value than the previous closing value. This is a typical scenario in the stock market, where price gaps/jumps between the closing price of one day and the opening price of the next day are often observed. These upward jumps indicate that the buyers are still trying to push the price upwards, but the sellers are again gaining the upper hand during the candlestick period. Individual candlesticks in the 3BC formation often resemble the Marubozu candlesticks and signal a strong downward impulse. If the buyers finally give up and if prices no longer jump upward, you can often observe a strong downward movement after the 3BC formation when only the sellers remain in the market.

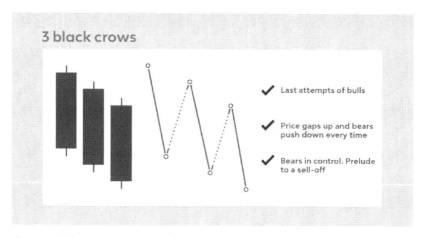

Figure 16: If you notice the 3 Black Crows, they often lead to a strong impulse movement as soon as the buyers withdraw from the market.

3.6.3 Three Inside Up (3IU)

The 3IU formation is another important formation with high information content. The second candlestick of this formation is a small candlestick, which is completely engulfed by the previous one, hence the term **inside**. This means that the price movement is slowing down.

The third candlestick is a strong impulse candlestick, which is similar to the Marubozu candlestick, with a long candlestick body. It ultimately confirms that the sellers have been completely pushed out of the market and that the market is now dominated by buyers.

The 3IU formation is a good example of how we can combine what we have learnt so far to analyse candlestick sequences effectively: If the candlesticks become smaller, they indicate that a trend is slowing down. Long shadows also signal a rejection and the strong impulse candlestick in the opposite direction of long shadows confirms the final change of direction.

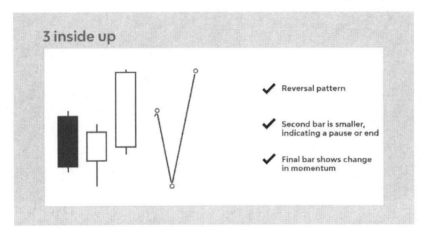

Figure 17: The inside-up candlestick is an effective reversal signal and it indicates the shifting strength ratio.

3.6.4 Evening Star/Abandoned Baby

There are various multiple candles patterns that are based on the Doji candlestick. However, their meaning is often similar, and considering only the most important Doji formation suffices in developing a general understanding of this pattern.

As already mentioned, a Doji is a neutral candlestick and only indicates a temporary pause in the price movement and equilibrium between the buyers and the sellers. But if a single Doji becomes part of a multiple candles pattern, we as traders can see interesting formations on our charts.

The Evening Star is a formation in which a Doji follows an upward trend candlestick. The Doji initially indicates only a temporary pause in the upward trend and has no significance on its own. However, if the Doji is followed by a strong Marubozu candlestick in the opposite trend direction, this often signals a complete trend reversal.

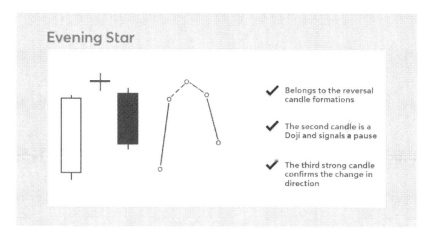

Figure 18: The Evening Star is a pattern based on the Doji candlestick. In this case, the Doji signals the market high during a trend phase and it is followed by a strong impulse into the opposite direction.

The Evening Star information, thus, describes the slowly reversing strength ratio in a trend movement. The Doji marks a turning point at which the price is too high for the buyers to continue buying, but is high enough for sellers to enter the market. The forces of buying and selling interests neutralise each other at the top of the Doji and then start their new trend movement when the sellers enter the market.

3.6.5 The element of "context"

Candlesticks independently offer a good starting point for analysing the prevailing strength ratios between the buyers and the sellers and for identifying possible trend reversal or trend continuation signals.

In my opinion, an effective analysis of candlesticks is, however, not sufficient to become a successful trader in the long run since it only provides an extremely limited cross-section of charts and neglects important chart context.

Based on what we have learnt until now, important concepts such as trend and momentum analyses will be explained below so that even the long-term chart cross-sections can be interpreted correctly.

3.6.6 Candlestick cheat sheets

All graphics have been comprehensibly compiled on www.tradeciety.com/candlesticks/. These can be printed and used in your own trading.

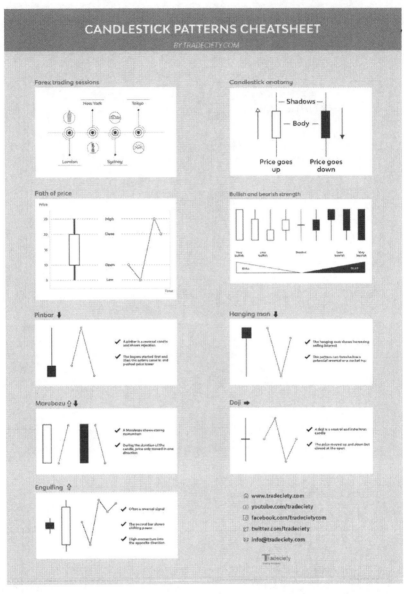

Figure 19: This cheat sheet and other information are available to readers. Use the link to get all details.

4. Chart anatomy

The next step in understanding technical charts is to explore the different chart formations. Classical chart formations can include dozens of candlesticks and, thus, carry even more information content.

Figure 20 illustrates how an engulfing candlestick formation on the Daily time frame (left) looks like a multi-candle Head-and-shoulder formation on the 1-H time frame (right). We will cover the Head & Shoulder formation in the next sections.

Owing to the larger context and extended information contents, the analysis of broad chart patterns is, therefore, informative for effective technical analysis. The aim of this chapter is to enable attentive readers to correctly interpret any chart in practice and to significantly exceed the analytical ability of most traders.

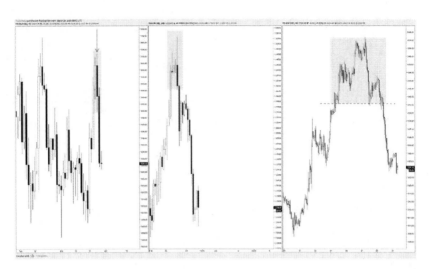

Figure 20: *We can see the daily chart on far left; the marked area in this chart represents an Engulfing candlestick. The 4-hour chart can be seen in the middle and it already contains more information. The Head-and-shoulders formation can be seen at the far right in this pattern on the 1-Hour chart. The more we zoom-in, the more information is visible.*

4.1 Chart phases

At any given time, the price can either rise, fall, or move sideways. This may sound simple, but as we have already seen during the candlestick analysis, we can quickly acquire comprehensive knowledge when we break down complex facts into its single components.

Figure 21 shows that each chart comprises the following five phases:

- **Trends**

    If the price rises over a period, it is called a rally, a bull market or just an upward trend. If the price falls continuously, it is called a bear market, a sell-off or a downward trend.

    Different trends can have varied degrees of intensity. In the next section, we will learn the individual facets of trend analysis.

- **Corrections**

    Corrections are short price movements against the prevailing trend direction. During an upward trend, corrections are short-term phases in which the price falls. As we will see, the price does not always move in a straight line in one direction during trend phases, but constantly moves up and down in so-called price waves.

- **Consolidations**

    Consolidations are sideways phases. During a sideways phase, the price moves sideways in a usually clearly defined price corridor and there are no impulses to start a trend.

- **Breakouts**

    The buyers and the sellers are in equilibrium during a sideways phase. If the strength ratio between the buyers and the sellers changes during consolidations and one side of the market players wins the majority, a breakout occurs from such a sideways phase. The price then starts a new trend. Breakouts are, therefore, a link between consolidations and new trends.

- **Trend reversal**

    If a correction continues for a long time and if its intensity increases, a correction can also lead to a complete trend reversal and initiate a new trend. Like breakouts, trend reversal scenarios, thus, signal a transition in prices from one market phase to the next.

Figure 21: *A classic example of the division of a complete price chart into the individual chart phases. This procedure is helpful for using the following concepts of technical analysis in the correct context.*

47

4.2 Application and chart analyses

The price charts in figures 21 and 22 show the different price phases. During the long-term trends, short correction phases, or consolidations, can be seen time and again. If a consolidation continues for a long time, it shows that the buyers and the sellers are in equilibrium and that the previous trend is coming to an end. If a breakout occurs, a new trend starts and the same pattern repeats.

The chart phases can be universally observed since they represent the battle between the buyers and the sellers. This concept is timeless and it describes the mechanism that causes all price movements. The trend phase pushes the price upwards, indicating the buyer overhang. The consolidations mark temporary trend pauses; however, a trend is continued until the price does not reach a new high during an upward trend. Corrections show the short-term increase of the opposition. If these are fended off, the trend continues its movement. On the other hand, long correction phases eventually develop into new trends when the strength ratio shifts completely.

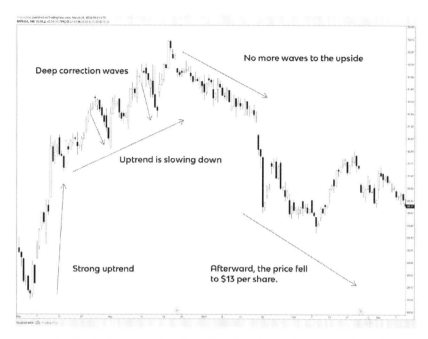

Figure 22: This chart cross-section shows the slow change from a buyer's market to a seller's market. The individual chart phases are clearly defined and each phase is driven by the so-called price waves.

Although the sequence and strength of individual chart phases can vary greatly, any chart contains only these phases. If we understand them comprehensively, price analysis becomes relatively simple.

4.3 Chart components

Similar to the candlestick analysis, it is also helpful to break down chart patterns into their individual components to understand complex facts more easily.

A closer look at the chart phases reveals that each phase can be characterised by only two features – **price waves** and **swing points**. In the following sections, price waves and swing waves are explained and analysed in the chart context.

4.3.1 Introduction to price waves

Price waves are the most important components available to technical traders, because every chart phase and every chart pattern can be clearly described using only price waves.

As already mentioned, the price on the charts usually does not move in a straight line from point A to point B, but always in an up and down fashion. These individual upward and downward movements represent the so-called **price waves**.

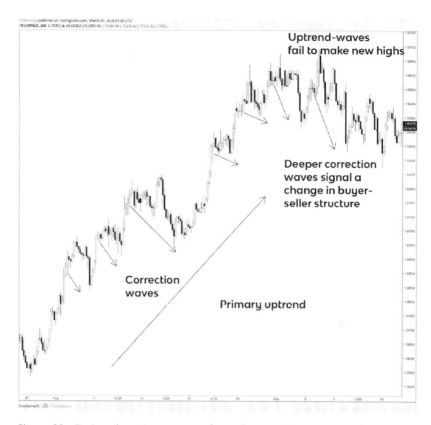

Figure 23: During the primary upward trend, correction waves in the opposite direction can be repeatedly observed. At the beginning, these are still short and not deep. If they become longer and deeper, e.g. at the right edge, this indicates that the buyers have lost their majority.

As already seen with the candlestick analysis, imaging all chart movements as a fight between the sellers and the buyers also helps in understanding the price waves.

In an **upward trend**, the upward price waves are steeper and longer than the downward correction price waves, because this is the only way for the price to move upwards. Buyers are therefore pushing up the price faster than the ability of sellers to resist this during the correction waves. The faster the price can rise during an uptrend, the greater the imbalance between buying and selling interest. The smaller the correction waves, compared to the trend waves, the stronger the trend is as well.

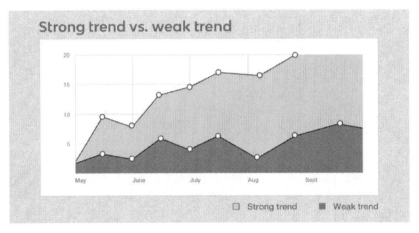

Figure 24: A strong trend has long trend waves and short correction waves and, thus, rises faster. A weak trend has a more balanced relationship between the trend waves and correction waves and, thus, rises flower.

In case of a **trend reversal**, like in figure 25, a shifting ratio between the upward and downward waves can be observed. If a chart changes from an upward trend to a downward trend, this means that the downward trend waves are more dominant now and the sellers have absorbed all the buying interest. A trend reversal is often preceded by longer correction waves that turn into new trend waves into the opposite direction. This indicates that the strength ratio has shifted.

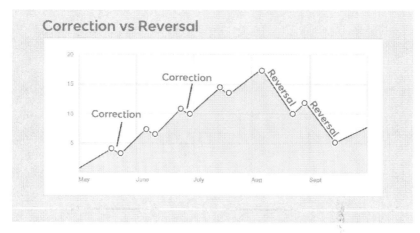

Figure 25: In case of a trend reversal, the correction wave becomes so long that they form new trend waves in the opposite direction.

During a **sideways market**, like in figure 26, the upward and downward price waves are equally strong and, hence, they neutralise each other. The buyers and the sellers are in equilibrium. The **breakout** then indicates that one side of the market participants has taken the initiative and is starting a new trend by absorbing all the interest. The breakout happens when the bullish trend waves, like in the example below, become longer and break the upper boundaries of a sideways market.

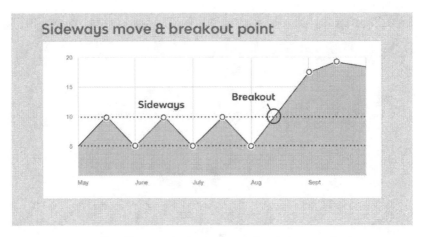

Figure 26: During the sideways phase, the upward and downward price waves are equally long. If a breakout occurs, new trend waves, which herald the upward trend, are formed.

4.3.2 Definition of swing points

The end points of price waves are also called **swing points**. Swing points offer us good supplementary aid for our chart analysis. If an upward trend wave comes to a temporary stop, for example if it is followed by a correction wave, then this is called a (swing) **high**. Likewise, the end point of a downward movement is also called the (swing) **low**.

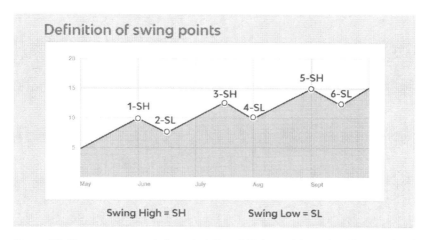

Definition of swing points

Swing High = SH   Swing Low = SL

Figure 27: The sequence and characteristics of highs and lows describe trend and sideways phases in the technical analysis. We can interpret any chart situation using them. HH stands for a higher high, HL is a higher low. Used in a downward trend

According to the classic trend definition, an upward trend can occur only if the price waves form **higher highs** and **higher lows**. A strong uptrend is characterized by rapidly rising swing highs and shallow swing lows.

Although this insight appears simple at first glance, it is the fundamental premise of technical analysis and even the **Dow theory**, developed around 1900, is based on this type of price analysis. The fact that it is still used today proves the timeless and universal principles of trend analysis.

Figure 28 shows the classic definition of trend movements using high and lows. During an upward trend on the left, the upward waves are longer and form correspondingly **higher highs** (1, 3, 5). The correction waves are shallow and the respective lows

(2, 4) are trending higher as well, confirming that the buying interest is predominant and absorbing all the selling interest earlier each time.

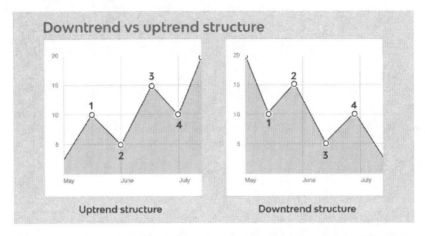

Figure 28: Classic Dow Theory defines an uptrend by higher highs and higher lows (right). A downtrend consists of lower lows and lower highs.

A trend reversal can be effectively described by using of highs and lows as shown in figure 29. If the price suddenly reaches a new lower low (6) and forms a lower high (5) during an upward trend, then the upward trend is broken according to the trend definition. A new downward trend can then emerge, because the sellers now have the upper hand and the downward trend waves are steeper and longer. The continuation of the upward trend has failed because it would have required a breakout above point 3.

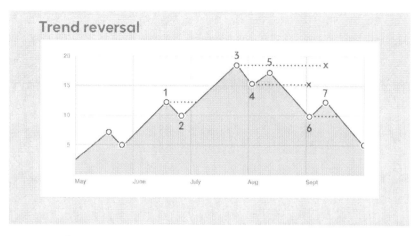

Figure 29: The trend reversal is confirmed if the price fails to reach a new high after point 5 and, at point 6, even sets a new low below 3.

Figure 30 shows a wheat price chart. The price starts in an upward trend on the left. Although some of the correction waves are pronounced, we do not see a break of a single (swing) low. The first break of a low occurs after the price at the peak has already formed lower highs and hinted declining buyer interest even before the actual break, marked with an X.

Figure 30: We can now effectively link price wave analysis to high and lows to understand any chart. Price waves and swing points are the building blocks of any chart and they build the foundation for all technical analysis.

4.4 Advanced wave analysis

Now, we are going even more granular. After seeing that any chart can only be made up of the various chart phases, which are made up of price waves themselves, we will explore the four different elements of wave analysis. Those conclude our foundational work. Every following chart formation, and any chart in general, can then be explained and understood with the previously learned building blocks.

4.4.1 Wave length

The length of the individual trend waves is the most important factor for assessing the strength of a price movement.

During an upward trend, long rising trend waves that are not interrupted by correction waves show that buyers have the majority. On the other hand, smaller trend waves or slowing trend waves show that a trend is not strong or is losing its strength. Figure 31 shows that the trending phases are clearly described by long price waves into the underlying trend direction.

Figure 31: Left: Long trend waves confirm the high trend strength. The trend comes to a standstill as soon as the waves shorten. Right: The downward trend is characterised by long falling trend waves. However, the length decreases downwards and the trend reverses shortly thereafter.

4.4.2 Angle / steepness

The rate with which the price rises during a trend is also of great importance. In general terms, moderate trends have a longer life span and a sudden increase in price usually indicates a less sustainable trend. We can often observe this phenomenon during so-called (price) bubbles, wherein the price falls again just as quickly after an explosive rise.

The development of the steepness of trends and price waves, compared to the overall chart context, is also important: Accelerating or weakening price waves might show that a trend is picking up speed or is slowly coming to a standstill.

60

Interesting correlations can be made together with the concept of length: A trend is intact if we find long trend waves or trend waves that become longer with a moderate or increasing angle. On the other hand, a trend with trend waves that become increasingly shorter, and which is simultaneously losing its steepness, indicates a possible imminent end. Figure 32 shows such a situation where the length and the steepness changed during the uptrend. The complete reversal soon followed.

Figure 32: The angle of the trend waves describes the strength of a trend. Decreasing angles and longer correction waves at the peak indicate the downward trend in advance.

4.4.3 Impulse vs. correction

If we add the ratio between the trend waves that move in the prevailing trend direction, the so-called impulsive waves, and correction waves as a third element to length and angle, we can understand almost every chart.

A trend with long trend waves and only short correction waves shows a greater imbalance between the buyers and the sellers. An upward trend with small correction waves signals that buying interest strongly outweighs selling interest and that the sellers have no great interest in current price developments or that the buyers immediately absorb all sellers.

A trend with longer correction waves which run deeper against the prevailing trend direction shows a different picture. Deep downward correction waves during an upward trend suggest that the sellers are active in the market and can move the price sharply in the meantime. This suggests that the strength ratio between the buyers and the sellers is more balanced. A trend like this is easier to turn, if the sellers become just a little stronger or the buyers withdraw a little. Thus, it always stands on the brink. The previous chart setup in figure 32 demonstrates how the downward trend was foreshadowed by an increase in size of the correction waves.

4.4.4 Swing structure

The swing structure refers to the formation of highs and lows. The interpretation is similar to the one of price waves.

For example, an intact upward trend usually manages effortlessly to set new highs. If the price has problems breaking through previous highs or does not manage to exceed the last ones, this may be a signal indicating that the trend will soon come to a standstill. Traders should be particularly watchful if the price immediately reverses after a breaking through a high and cannot continue to move in the trend direction. Such a trend weakness and it can often be a sign of **exhaustion**.

A complete break of a swing structure is often a clear sign indicating that the current trend is over. If the price does not break through the previous high and if the price falls even below the previous low, the upward trend is over. As soon as the price reaches a new low during an upward trend, the prevailing trend is over. In figure 33 the price first made a lower low during the uptrend (first X). This is already a strong bearish signal. Shortly after, the price also failed to make a new higher high (second X) and the complete trend reversal followed.

Figure 33: As already mentioned, trends and trend waves can be effectively analysed using high and lows. The points marked with X indicate the reversal of the highs and lows. First the price forms a new low (LL – lower low) and then the price does not manage to set a new high (LH – lower high).

We set up the URL www.tradeciety.com/waves/ which contains additional chart analyses and all cheat sheets from this chapter.

5. The most important chart patterns

Although I have said it many times during this book, it is worth repeating because it demonstrates the optimal approach for understanding technical analysis: not only do mindless memorisation and stereotyped template-thinking make little sense, but it also prevents traders from understanding the overall context. This kind of trading is restricted to only a few situations. Furthermore, traders like this, who learn by rote, are completely lost when they suddenly realise that the financial markets do not always follow their textbook formations and they lack the knowledge to deal with these unknown situations.

The following sections describe how to understand classical chart patterns based on the analysis tools that you have already learnt and how to apply the knowledge of elements like price waves, trends and price analyses to any other chart.

5.1 The Head-and-shoulders (HAS) formation

The Head-and-shoulders formation is an ideal introduction since what it communicates about the market activity and the balance between the buyers and the sellers is immediately clear, even without prior charting knowledge.

A Head-and-shoulders formation (HAS) is best sought during an established trend since it usually indicates a trend reversal scenario. The price waves at the left shoulder, and then at the head, confirm the conventional trend structure since they form higher highs. The right shoulder is the first lower high point and it indicates that buyers are no longer as strongly represented in the market.

If you connect the lows of the correction waves, you will get the so-called **neckline**. A break of this neckline after the right shoulder confirms that the price is now at a first lower low point and, thus, signals the end of the upward trend. The HAS formation rings in the new downward trend with the break of the neckline. Figure 34 illustrates the shift in the trend structure with a clear HAS formation.

It is important to wait for a **confirmed breakout** to avoid false signals. It can be often observed that the neckline is tested several times and rejections occur repeatedly at this neckline. The battle between the buyers and the sellers is intense at these points and many traders use such price levels to execute trades or place their trading orders.

I use different variations of the HAS formation and we will explore a few now. It is the cornerstone of one of my own trading strategies.

Figure 34: A classic Head-and-shoulders pattern at the end of an upward trend rings in the downward trend with the break of the neckline when price makes a first lower low.

5.1.1 Variations of the HAS formation

To move away from stereotyped thinking even further, it's worth considering a few variations of the HAS formation and thereby also the variations of the trend analysis.

5.1.1.1 Small heads and weak shoulders

If a deep correction wave follows the left shoulder before the price forms the head, it may already be an indication that there is increasing interest in selling and that the buyers are no longer dominant. The deeper the correction waves during an established trend, the stronger is the opposition. The impulse wave to the head in figure 35 below is short and also indicates that the buyers are not absolutely dominant anymore.

When the peak point of the right shoulder is formed far below the head, like in the chart scenario below, this further confirms that the buyers can no longer move the price up.

Figure 35: The move up into the head is short. The right shoulder is barely developed and further indicates that there is little interest in buying. The sell-off was foreshadowed by those characteristics.

Figure 36 shows that the distance between the peak of the left shoulder and the head is relatively small. This indicates that the majority of the buyers has moved away from the market and the price can no longer rise as easily as before.

Figure 36: The last price wave towards the head is very small and hardly manages to form a new high. The subsequent break of the neckline follows with a lot of momentum, since the market has no buyers any longer.

5.1.1.2 Break of the neckline and the retest

The break of the neckline is usually the entry signal for most traders, because it completes the HAS formation. The break confirms that the price makes a lower high at the right shoulder and it forms the first lower low as well. Those two points signal a trend change based on the Dow Theory as well.

The stronger the break and the more impulsive the price wave that breaks through the neckline, the higher the probability that the new downward trend will continue.

An alternative entry signal is given when the price moves back to the neckline from below and conducts a so-called **retest**. If the trend structure remains intact and the price does not manage to move above this point, the HAS formation can indicate the second entry point. This retest shows that the buyers have once again tried to increase the price, but ultimately did not have the power to achieve this. The sellers defended the high and took the opportunity to get into the market at an even better price one last time. Subsequently, a rapid drop in price can often be observed when buyers completely withdraw from the market.

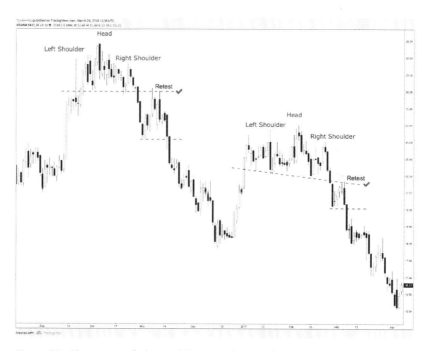

Figure 37: The retest of the neckline is a frequently observed pattern that can provide an additional trade signal.

5.1.2 Inverse HAS formations

The inverse HAS formation is the counterpart of the regular HAS formation and can be observed during a downward trend. The idea is the same: After a downward trend with lower lows that form the left shoulder and the head, the right shoulder is the first higher low that indicates a slowly changing buyer-seller ratio. If the subsequent price wave then also breaks the neckline upwards, it confirms the start of a new bullish trend.

The variations and the retest principles are similar to those of the regular HAS formation.

Figure 38: The inverse Head-and-shoulders formation is observed at the end of a downward trend. The new upward trend starts after breaking the neckline. Here we can also see a retest of the neckline as well.

5.2 Cup and Handle

The "Cup and Handle" (CAH) formation describes the slowly reversing market sentiment effectively as well.

The CAH formation is often preceded by an upward trend. The uptrend then flattens and the price even falls when it forms the **left half of the cup**. However, the downward trend is not pronounced and the **right half of the cup** shows the initiation of another uptrend phase once again. The rounded-off pattern can arise only when the price gradually moves from the lower highs and lows to the higher highs and lows. You can clearly see the slow change of trend direction during the cup in figure 39.

When the price returns to the previous high, which formed the **left edge of the cup**, there is usually no direct breakout; instead, the price drops again for a short time and the cup **handle** is formed. However, the handle indicates only a brief correction phase and the buyers return quickly to push the price upwards.

The averted downward trend of the cup already indicates that the buyers are slowly gaining the majority. The final signal with the CAH formation is given when the price breaks the handle to the upside.

The CAH formation is, thus, classified as a trend continuation formation since the previous upward trend is only briefly interrupted during the cup phase and the sellers' attempt to reverse the trend is fended off.

Figure 39: The Cup and Handle formation is a breakout or trend continuation formation. The handle indicates that the buyers immediately push the price back to the same high and the breakout then indicates the trend continuation.

5.3 Ascending triangle

The ascending triangle is also a trend continuation formation. During an upward trend, it indicates a temporary consolidation before the price continues the trend.

This formation has two important characteristics which indicate that the buyers still have the majority. Firstly, the price always manages to return to the same high, which means that the sellers do not have great interest in catching up with the price earlier. Secondly – and this point is the most important part of the ascending triangle – the lows show an upward trend, i.e. the buyers push up the price earlier with each downward movement and the sellers cannot raise enough interest to form a new lower low. The two chart studies in figure 40 show how the ascending triangle looks on an actual price chart.

If the sellers finally withdraw from the market, there will be an upward breakout and the upward trend will continue at a higher high. The breakout point, or when the price closes outside the triangle, is the entry signal for most traders.

The focus should be on the angles of the trend lines (the diagonal price lines), because if we can interpret these correctly, we can also read numerous other chart situations. The way the price moves to a high or a low says a lot about the prevailing ratio between the buyers and the sellers.

Figure 40: *The ascending triangle is a trend continuation signal and it shows that the price is repeatedly pushing into the same highs. The lows are already rising and indicate increasing buyer interest.*

5.4 Wedges

Although the wedges are similar to triangles, they are not like the consolidation patterns. Wedges are normally trend reversal formations, i.e. a wedge often indicates the end of a dominant trend.

5.4.1 Classical wedge

Figure 41 shows a classical wedge formation. During the upward trend, the price moves in a narrowing area towards the end of the wedge. Even if the price is still rising, the flatter angle of the rising highs indicates that the buyers no longer have a significant surplus. The price rises slower and slower. Towards the end of the wedge, there are no clear trend waves any longer, and we can only observe narrow price movements. All this indicates an end of the trend.

If it then leads to a downward breakout, the sell signal is given. The price now makes lower lows and lower highs. Figure 41 shows a wedge during an upward trend. It is obvious that the uptrend slowed down during the formation of the wedge. The X marks the final breakout point and the trigger point of the wedge pattern.

Figure 41: The wedge indicates that the trend waves converge at the peak of the formation. The highs do not rise significantly which indicates the dwindling buying interest.

The same principles apply to the reverse variant: If we see a wedge during a downward trend, like in figure 42, wherein the lows flatten out and the price no longer pushes down as easily, it indicates that the sellers are losing their majority. In a wedge, we can often notice rejection candles, where long downward shadows indicate failed attempts to continue the downward trend. All this points to a slowly reversing balance between the buyers and the sellers. The upward outbreak then completes this trend reversal formation.

Figure 42: This chart analysis shows a wedge at the end of a downward trend. The candlestick with a long downward shadow further confirms the rejection and leads to a strong change to the upside when the sellers completely withdraw.

5.4.2 The wedge as a trend continuation

The example in figure 43 shows a wedge that has formed during a correction phase in an overall downward trend. The wedge phase is marked with dotted lines. Although the wedge shows higher highs and higher lows, the highs flatten and the buyers cannot get the upward trend to work.

Such a wedge formation becomes a continuation when the price fails to make a new high. The downward trend continues when the wedge is broken to the downside and the price continues to make lower lows. The continuation point is marked with an X in figure 43. Sometimes, such a pattern is also referred to as a **flag**.

Figure 43: Wedges can also appear as trend continuation formations. Initially, these look like possible reversal signals, but the highs do not rise significantly, indicating low buyer interest. If the wedge breaks, the trend continues.

Naturally, the same applies to a falling wedge in an upward trend as shown in figure 44. Although we can see lower highs and lows during the wedge, the new lows are weak and the sellers do not have the majority to start a strong downward trend. At the end of the wedge, the price fails to make a convincing new low. In the previous section about wave analysis, we learned that such a situation indicates a slowing trend. The downward trend is fended off when the price breaks higher and makes a new high, as indicated by the X in figure 44. The uptrend can then be resumed and traders looking for trend-trading opportunities use such breakout points to time their trades.

Figure 44: This wedge looks like a deep correction wave in an overall uptrend. The lows at the end of the wedge are no longer able to drop further. If it leads to a breakout, the upward trend continues.

5.5 Double and triple top

Double and triple tops are common; they are one of the most popular formations in technical analysis and it's easy to misinterpret them. An attentive and well-educated trader, however, can use those patterns to find trading opportunities.

Figure 45 shows that the price is repeatedly trying to break the last high (1) during an upward trend. The price fails every time and is pushed lower multiple times at points 2 and 3. This could indicate a lack of interest by the buyers and increasing selling interest. The double and triple top is, therefore, a trend reversal formation. If buyers then withdraw completely from the market and give up trying to break the high, a new downward trend usually starts.

The signal at the double and triple top is given when the price breaks out of the pattern and forms a new low. The X in figure 45 marks this breakout point.

Figure 45: *After the upward trend, the buyers try three times to break out the price upwards before the sellers reverse the trend after the breakout from the triple top.*

5.5.1 Retests

Like the Head-and-shoulders formation, the so-called retest often takes place at double tops/lows after the initial breakout.

Figure 46 shows a triple top and a triple bottom formation. After the breakout upwards, the price does not rise immediately, but it returns to the upper edge of the structure one last time. The arrow in figure 46 marks this retest point. Traders can find a second entry signal here and if the previous highs hold, an uptrend is often continued.

Figure 46: *This chart analysis shows a sideways movement with three highs and three lows. The high finally breaks out and the price then undergoes a retest before the upward trend is continued.*

I put together a video at www.tradeciety.com/patterns where you can learn more about the mentioned chart formations and how to track them on your charts.

6. Additional charting concepts

We can analyse and understand any price chart using the knowledge we have acquired so far. The following chapters focus on additional concepts of technical analysis that are helpful in identifying better trading opportunities and increasing the quality of trades.

6.1 Trend lines

Trend lines are tools that describe trends. But they can do much more, as we will see below.

6.1.1 Drawing the trend lines

Trend lines are usually drawn on the charts by connecting the lows in an upward trend and the highs during a downward trend. There are different approaches to drawing trend lines, but the outlined approach offers a robust charting methodology.

A confirmed trend line normally requires at least **three contact points** with the price. We can always connect any two random points on the charts, but the trend line is an active trend line only if we have a third contact point.

In addition, we must ensure our trend line does not excessively cut through the candlesticks. Trend lines that go through candlestick bodies should be avoided, whereas a trend line passing through candlestick shadows may be OK under specific circumstances. It is not always possible to describe a trend with a trend line and if the chart does not offer one, we should not force it.

The trend in figure 47 allows us to draw a trend line by connecting the lows. The trend line is confirmed on the third contact point and the fourth contact point provides another confirmation signal.

Trend lines are used by trend traders and reversal traders alike. Trend traders look for subsequent bounces to enter trades into the trend direction. The contact point 4 in figure 47 shows such an example.

Reversal traders wait for a confirmed breakout through the trend lines, anticipating a change in trend direction.

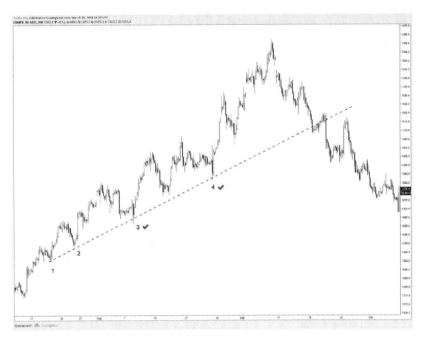

Figure 47: *Trend lines are tools to describe trend phases. You need at least three contact points to confirm the trend lines.*

6.1.2 Trend line angle

As already mentioned, the slope of the trend waves indicates whether a trend is gaining or losing strength.

The so-called **bump-and-run formation** comprises two parts: The trend progresses moderately in the initial phase, namely the **lead-in phase**. If the trend intensifies and the price moves away from the previous trend line, the **bump phase** is reached.

It is well known that trends can lose their sustainability quickly if the price rises too fast. This mechanism builds the foundation for the bump-and-run formation. If we see a significant increase in the angles of trend lines, we should be careful. The signal for a trend reversal and the **run phase** can be noticed when the price breaks the steeper trend line or when the price forms a new low as shown in figure 48.

Figure 48: The chart analysis shows an increasingly rapid upward trend with rising trend lines. During the bump phase, the stock has risen almost vertically, indicating bubble characteristics. If the price breaks the low and the trend line, a downward trend is likely to start.

The other trend line signal is given when trends with low or declining angles form on your charts. If the price moves slowly in one direction and the angle is extremely flat, this may indicate that market players do not fully support the trend and the ratio between buyers and sellers is more balanced. This prevents the price from rising or falling faster. Wedges are an example of this phenomenon as we have seen previously.

The left trend line in figure 49 shows a scenario wherein the upward trend rises only slowly with a small angle. This indicates that although the buyers are in control, the buying interest does not significantly predominate. A slight shift can cause a trend reversal when the selling interest absorbs all the buying interest. The break of the trend line confirms that the direction changes.

The subsequent downward trend shows how flattening trend lines can point to the end of a trend as well. The sellers are gradually losing the upper hand and the ratio between the buyers and the sellers is becoming more and more balanced. This characteristic also builds the foundation of the wedge pattern as we have seen previously.

Figure 49: The downward trend on the right side flattens out as indicated by the trend lines and the smaller slope.

Excursus: Confluence

If two or more formations, patterns or signals such as wedges, candlestick patterns and trend lines occur together, the signal force of different concepts is combined. This is called **confluence** in technical analysis.

The signal strength of a trading situation normally increases when more confluence factors are combined.

When analysing chart patterns, combining individual candlestick patterns with broader chart formations has proven to be helpful. An example of this is a rejection or engulfing candlestick at the end of a double low – the spring pattern.

As already mentioned, technical analysis works, among other things, because millions of market players use it and it leads to a self-fulfilling prophecy. Not every trader will follow the Head-and-shoulders formation or use trend lines or candlestick patterns, but if several patterns and signals are clubbed together, more traders will become aware of them and then draw the same conclusions, increasing the probability of a successful trading opportunity.

6.1.3 Trend line breaks

A powerful trading signal is generated when an active trend line is broken. This often foreshadows a change in the trend direction and it confirms a shift in the market structure.

Figure 50 shows various confirmed trend lines with more than three contact points in each case. A break of a trend line always initiates a new trend. Interestingly, every break of a trend line is preceded by a change in the highs and lows first. When the price breaks a trend line during an upward trend, we can often notice how the trend has already formed lower highs.

The break of the trend line is then the final signal, whereupon the trend reversal is initiated.

Figure 50: *Broken confirmed trend lines can be good trading opportunities. Before the breaks, we can often see that the highs and lows have already changed as marked with various Xs.*

6.1.4 Subjectivity of trend lines

Traders can get into trouble quickly because it is not always obvious how a trend line can be drawn. If there are uncertainties in the correct application of the trend lines, it is advisable to combine them with horizontal breakouts. This makes trading more objective. Thus, do not trade at the first signal when the price breaks the trend line, but only when the price subsequently forms a new low or high as well. These signals usually occur in quick succession, and hence the trader does not have to wait too long for his/her signal, but can nevertheless improve the quality of his/her trading and, at the same time, integrate another confluence factor into his/her trading.

6.2 Support and resistance

Support and resistance are other important trading concepts that are used by most trading strategies in some form. Support and resistance are ideal tools to identify important price levels and use them as additional confluence factors.

6.2.1 Drawing support and resistance

Support and resistance are price levels at which the price has previously shown a reversal reaction. Thus, a **resistance** zone is an area in which an upward trend has previously come to a standstill and has undergone a downward trend reversal. A **support** level is an area where a past downward trend has not generated enough selling interest and the trend has reversed upwards.

The upper line in figure 51 represents a resistance level. The lower line is a support level.

Like the trend lines, the rule with the three contact points applies here as well. A good support and resistance zone is confirmed only when the price has returned to it three times and has shown a reaction.

Figure 51: Support and resistance levels *are important reversal points on the charts.*

6.2.2 The idea behind support and resistance

Support and resistance indicate important price levels, because if the price is repeatedly forced to turn at the same level, this level must be significant and is used by many market players for their trading decisions.

If an upward trend is repeatedly forced to reverse at the same resistance, this means that the ratio between the buyers and the sellers suddenly tips over. Not only do all buyers withdraw at once, but the sellers immediately dominate the market activity when they start the new downward trend.

97

6.2.3 Support and resistance as trend reversal

There are several options for including the concept of support and resistance in actual trading decisions.

Traditionally, support and resistance are used to identify prices which are prone to a trend reversal, even in the future. If the price is in an upward trend and then approaches a previous resistance level, many traders will wait to trade another downward trend reversal from such a level. To increase the chances of a successful trading opportunity, do not blindly enter trades in such support and resistance areas. It is advisable to wait for more confluence factors. For example, if a head-and-shoulders formation or a double top appear at a support and resistance level, then this can increase the chances of a positive result.

Figure 52 shows how the left head-and-shoulders pattern occurred right at a long-term resistance level on the right. Point 4 on the right chart marks where the head-and-shoulders forms. Zooming in and out on your chart can often help to see the bigger picture better and enable you pick up important clues.

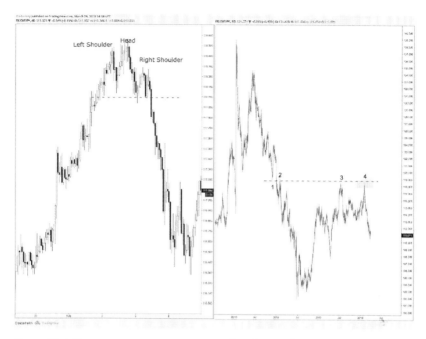

Figure 52: When we zoom out, we can see that the Head-and-shoulders formation forms directly at the lower end of the strong resistance level, creating additional confluence for our trade.

6.2.4 Support and resistance order absorption

Naturally, support and resistance do not always stop the price from continuing a trend. Breakouts can provide high probability trading signals as well.

The conventional technical analysis says: The more often the price reaches a certain level of support or resistance, the stronger it becomes. However, I cannot fully agree with this.

Every time the price reaches a support or resistance level, the balance between the buyers and the sellers changes. Whenever the price reaches resistance during an upward trend, more sellers will enter the market and enter their sell trades. If the price reaches the same resistance level again, fewer sellers will wait there. This phenomenon is also called **order absorption**. The resistance is gradually weakened until the buyers no longer encounter resistance and the price can break out upward and continue the upward trend.

We can observe this phenomenon when the rejections from a resistance become increasingly weaker and the price can return to the resistance level more quickly in each case. Formations such as triangles or the Cup and Handle are based on the concept of order absorption as well.

Figure 53 shows such an example. The Silver price returns sooner and sooner to the same resistance level, as the arrows indicate. This suggests that fewer sellers are interested in selling at the resistance level each time. In this case, the resistance level becomes increasingly weaker. Furthermore, just before the breakout occurred, the trend was accelerating upwards as the dotted arrow indicates. Eventually, the price broke through the resistance level and an extended upward trend emerged when no selling interest was left.

Figure 53: The order absorption phenomenon can be observed in the chart. The resistance level is gradually weakened each time the price came back to it.

6.2.5 Levels vs. zones

The price is an extremely dynamic concept. The classic concept of individual thin price lines that represent support and resistance is often little helpful and many traders fail using support and resistance tools for this reason. Therefore, I always recommend using support and resistance **zones** to get a better explanation.

Figure 54 shows a price chart with conventional price lines as support and resistance. At first glance, this looks promising and the impact and reversal points can be clearly seen.

Figure 54: The support and resistance lines look effective at defining price reversal points at first glance.

On closer inspection, it however becomes clear that the price lines are mostly not respected at all and the price tends to either miss or overshoot these lines as shown in figure 55. This regularly leads to great frustration for traders who either miss potentially profitable trades by a narrow margin or are forced to exit too early due to stop runs. If a trader misses a trade, he/she tends to be more aggressive next time. And if he/she gets taken out too soon, he/she will be too careless with the trade exits next time. Traders, who follow this pattern, are always in a reactive mode and their trading is inconsistent, which can lead to major errors and overall bad trading behaviour.

Figure 55: On closer inspection, it is noticeable that the price rarely respects the lines exactly and often overshoots or reverses early.

Figure 56 shows that a trader is better advised to mark support and resistance areas using zones to increase the explanatory value of those concepts. The zones help in filtering out noise and premature signals. The zones may appear broad at first glance, but a trader would treat such a zone as a noise corridor and stay away from trading within those zones.

This procedure is also ideal for the so-called **multi-time-frame analysis**, which is used to identify important price levels in the higher time frames and then go to a lower time frame to wait for further confluence factors in the lower time frame.

In this case, the trader would use the zones he/she identified on the Daily time frame and then look for trading opportunities on the intraday time frames.

Figure 56: We should form zones in order to increase the explanatory value of support and resistance and to filter out the price noise.

6.3 Supply and demand zones

The concept of supply and demand zones is similar to that of support and resistance, and even the application is analogous. However, there are a few important differences as well which enable traders to use both concepts simultaneously to find high impact price areas.

6.3.1 The idea behind supply and demand zones

Supply and demand zones are usually relatively narrow price corridors in which the price has initially paused briefly before it exploded in one direction and started a strong trend.

In these supply and demand zones, the ratio between the buyers and the sellers tilts so rapidly that the price moves away from these zones in an extremely impulsive manner.

Figure 57 below demonstrates the behaviour of a demand zone nicely. For example, if there is a sudden and strong upward breakout in a demand zone (1), it shows that the buyers suddenly absorb all selling interest. This imbalance usually occurs in valid demand zones without notice from one moment to the next, which confirms that buying interest in this zone has accumulated in a flash and that all sellers have withdrawn at once. If the price enters such a demand zone again (x), buying interest still exists probably because not all market players managed to enter the market during the first movement. Traders, who follow the concept of demand zones, will therefore look for clues and other confluence factors in these zones to trade during the next upward movement.

Figure 57: At point 1, we suddenly see a strong, explosive breakout, which indicates a significant overweight of buyers. We call this a demand zone. If the price falls back into this zone, the left-over buying interest is picked up and price can start a new upwards trend once again.

There are several methods to identify supply and demand on the charts. The five most important factors are:

1. **Moderate volatility**

   Good supply and demand zones are usually relatively narrow and the price does not fluctuate strongly during the short consolidation phase. This indicates a proper balance.

2. **Timely breakout**

   Good zones should not wait too long for the breakout and the consolidation phases are often short. The underlying idea is that the buying and selling interests suddenly tilt, but this imbalance ought not to be too long in coming.

   Figure 58 shows a newly created supply area on the left. The price did not spend much time during the initial consolidation phase going sideways and the breakout was extremely strong. Those characteristics confirm the supply zone. The next time the price entered the zone, it lead to a new sell off. The X marks the point of the re-entry into the supply zone.

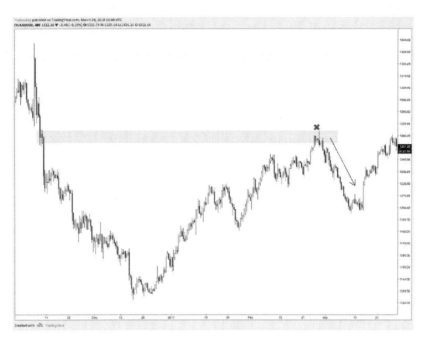

Figure 58: *The supply zone on the left extends over only two candlesticks before the price breaks out with a strong momentum. In case of a re-entry, the open interest in selling is picked up and the price drops again (X).*

3. Strong breakout

The strong breakout is the most important feature: The stronger the breakout away from the initial zone, the higher the probability of the price showing such a reaction in case of the next entry.

Figure 59 shows a strong supply zone on the left. The breakout away from the zone was explosive and lead to a steep downward trend. The price returned to the supply area twice, as indicated by the Xs. Each time, a new sell-off was initiated.

Figure 59: The downward breakout out of the supply zone on the left happens from one candlestick to the next without any notice or sign. This indicates a strong imbalance and marks an important supply zone. In case of a re-entry, the price again falls two times due to the great interest in selling (Xs).

Figure 60 shows a demand zone. Suddenly, at point 1 on the left, the price strongly moved upwards after a downward trend. This strong reversal upward indicates a strong reaction and can suggest a lot of buying interest in the area.

The price returned to the demand zone twice (point 2 and 3) and completely reversed upward each time. As indicated by the initial demand zone reaction at point 1, the buying interest absorbs all selling interest immediately.

109

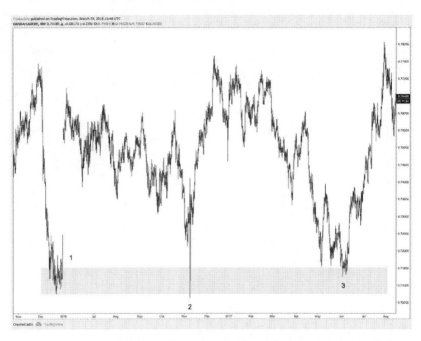

Figure 60: At point 1, the demand zone is created and the buyer overhang is so large that the price jumps up by hundreds of points. At point 2, although the zone is initially overshot, the upward reversal represents a strong reaction zone and again indicates a significant imbalance. At point 3 the pending buying interest is filled again and the upward trend starts anew.

4. Order absorption

The concept of order absorption, which we have learnt in connection with support and resistance, says: price levels can be weakened with each contact point.

Therefore, only the first, or at most the second, re-entry into a supply and demand zone should be traded.

With each re-entry, increasingly more buying or selling interest that still exists is utilised until the zone is no longer significant.

5. Spring formation

This confluence factor cannot always be found in a supply or demand zone, but it can improve the quality of such a zone. A spring formation shows a failed breakout attempt, which is immediately reversed.

Figure 61 shows a supply zone with a spring pattern on the left. The price has tried to break out upward, but the breakout attempt was fended off immediately. The sellers have immediately reversed the complete trend, resulting in an explosive downward trend. The imbalance between the buyers and the sellers must therefore be particularly large in such an area. Each time the price re-entered the supply zone afterward, a new downward trend was initiated.

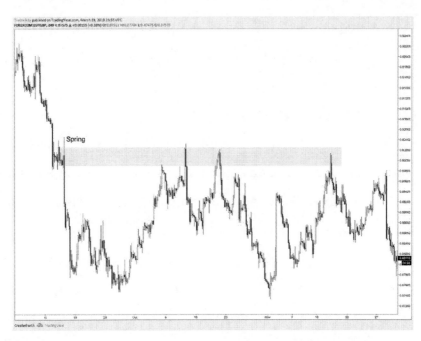

Figure 61: *The supply zone on the left is accompanied by a spring formation; during the subsequent price movement, several sales reactions can be seen, confirming the strength of the demand zone.*

6.4 Traps

Those who have a little more trading experience are probably familiar with the situation where a trade looked obvious at first, but then the opposite happens immediately. In retrospect, it is often quickly apparent that you have fallen into the same trap again and entered the market too early. Understanding how this can happen and what can be done about it is an important step on the way to become a successful trader.

6.4.1 Mechanisms of a buyer trap

To understand what happens in a trap, the interaction between the buyers and the sellers must be analysed precisely. The following chart situation (figure 62) illustrates this well.

1. Initially, the price moves lower in a normal downward trend. Many traders might have missed this trend and, thus, also missed the profit opportunities. Now, they are impatiently waiting for the next entry opportunity.
2. The price makes another swing low. According to classic Dow Theory, traders will now wait for a break of such a low to get into a short trade.
3. The price breaks the low and drops a little, which gives a good feeling to the traders who are now shorting. It also induces other traders to join when they see the price has

fallen below the low. We can often observe that these breakouts start strongly at the beginning, which also attracts the other breakout traders and makes this trap look attractive.

4. The price suddenly turns up and the trap snaps. In case of extremely effective traps, this spontaneous reversal after the breakout usually happens in only one candlestick or with a price jump. The downward outbreak is often initiated by professional traders and as soon as they see that the trap snaps and the amateur traders place their sell trades, they enter into buying trades to position themselves for the reversal.

5. The upward trend is now accelerating and traders with the sell positions are suddenly facing large losses. However, to end their sell trades, they must buy, which then further accelerates the upward price movement.

Figure 62: The mechanisms of the price trap and failed breakouts are evident from this Crude Oil chart.

6.4.2 How to avoid traps

Naturally, it is not always possible to avoid a trap and occasional loss trades are quite normal. However, an experienced trader can often avoid these traps by observing the following two points.

1. Avoid late entries

Traps usually occur after long trend phases. Traders, who follow trends, should avoid or be careful about entering a trend late. A trend that has already formed four or five trend waves is more likely to reverse. This is especially applicable when a flattening trend or a wedge is already noticeable.

2. Wait for confirmed breakouts

Most traps can be avoided by trading only in case of confirmed breakouts. Do not jump on the emerging breakout attempts. It is, therefore, advisable to wait for the completion of candlesticks to make trading decisions. Waiting until a candlestick has completely broken through the previous high or low and has closed outside it, can greatly reduce the probability of falling into a trap. It tests your patience and the greed-responses kick in, but waiting the confirmation is the better strategy long-term.

However, if you realise that you have fallen into a trap, you should admit this and close your losing trade to avoid further problems.

6.4.3 Double bottom trap

Double tops are often ideal areas to observe and trade price traps. Many traders trade breakouts at these price levels. Owing to the general impatience of traders, which usually leads to early trade entries, traps are effective at double tops.

Traps also occur repeatedly in support and resistance zones when traders trade breakouts too early and the price falls back again. The more obvious such a potential breakout is, the more common traps are.

As already mentioned, the spring formation is an effective confluence factor that can strengthen a trap. The stronger the rejection signal of the spring candlestick, the more effective is such a trap since many trades were withdrawn from here.

Figure 63 shows such an example. The price tried to break out higher during the uptrend. The price was immediately reversed after the weak breakout attempt, creating a trap. The price then sold off because the selling interest absorbed all the buying interest, following the trap.

Figure 63: *Various confluence factors announce the downward trend effectively: The failed breakout attempt takes place after a long consolidation phase and the price then also breaks through the last lows and through the trend line.*

6.4.4 Failed breakouts

Effective trap formations can be observed around double tops and double bottoms when the patterns are accompanied by the **spring** pattern. In figure 64 the spring pattern is a single candle formation that indicates a failed upward breakout attempt through a previous swing high point. Ideally, the spring candle has a long upward shadow, which marks the averted breakout and confirms the rejection. The rejection shows that the price initially tries to rise, but it is then reversed by the selling interest.

118

More aggressive and risk-seeking traders can use the spring candle as a direct entry signal to enter their sell trades earlier. Risk-averse traders wait for additional confirmation and usually enter trades when the price breaks through the previous support and makes lower lows.

Figure 64: The spring formation is a failed breakout attempt. This indicates that there are not enough buyers in the market. The continuation of the downward trend was indicated in advance by the spring formation.

7. School of indicators

Technical analysis includes not only candlestick patterns and chart formations, but also the so-called indicators.

7.1 What are indicators?

Indicators are tools that analyse the price using certain formulae and support us in our decision-making through direct visual evaluations on our charts. The indicators usually analyse the characteristics of candlestick opening and closing prices, the size and development of candlesticks and the ratio between the buyer and the seller candlesticks to obtain information regarding current market proceedings and the prevailing strength ratio.

7.1.1 Indicator lagging – are indicators too slow?

Many traders have prejudices against indicators and claim that they are not helpful because they are only based on the price information that is already available and therefore do not contribute anything new to chart analysis. In this context, the keyword **lagging** is often used by traders to suggest that the information from indicators lags behind the price and gives signals too late since they are based on past data.

I cannot agree with this. The same criticism would then have to be made against candlesticks and chart patterns, since we can recognise a candlestick or a chart pattern only when the price has already moved and we look at past information. However, this does not make technical analysis or the use of indicators any less valuable. If a trader knows how to interpret the information on his/her charts correctly, lagging is often attributed to pure ignorance of inexperienced or poorly trained traders.

In the following section, we will see how indicators can be used correctly and effectively to improve the quality of our own trading significantly.

7.1.2 Indicator groups

There are numerous indicators that can be ultimately divided into three indicator groups:

1. **Momentum indicators**

   Momentum indicators are often known as oscillators since they oscillate between the defined upper and lower limits. They help us in analysing the ratio of the buyers and sellers to understand which group of market players have the majority and how strongly the candlesticks are pushing in one direction or whether the price is losing strength.

2. **Trend indicators**

Trend indicators analyse a prevailing trend. They are generally not effective when the price enters a sideways phase, but can be important tools in trend markets.

3. Volatility indicators

The group of indicators checks the degree of volatility and the extent to which the price fluctuates. This information is usually needed to place trades, set stops, define goals and determine the position size.

Momentum	Trend	Volatility	Chart studies
Stochastic	ADX	Bollinger Bands®	Horizontal lines
RSI	Moving averages	Standard deviation	Fibonacci
CCI		ATR	Supply / Demand
Williams %	MACD	Keltner Channel	Trend lines
MACD	Parabolic SAR	Envelopes	
	Bollinger Bands®		
	Ichimoku Cloud		

7.1.3 Indicator selection and redundancy

The most important factor for selecting the indicators is to use only one indicator per group to avoid repeat (redundant) signals. For example, if a trader uses two or more momentum indicators, they will always show him/her the same signals, which may have a significant impact on his/her decision-making. The trader will then give too much importance to individual signals because he/she thinks that suddenly all indicators give the same signal to buy or sell, although they are only redundant signals.

7.2 Moving averages

Moving averages (MA) are by far the most popular indicators used by numerous traders and are even used in the mainstream financial media.

7.2.1 What is the function of moving averages?

Moving averages (MA) indicate an average price. If an MA is set to 14 periods, it shows the average price over the last 14 periods (or 14 candlesticks). The average price is important because it shows whether the current price is above or below the average and whether it is cheap or expensive compared to the past.

7.2.2 Which MA is the best – EMA or SMA?

There are many types of MA and hence the question arises which is the best one. The EMA (Exponential Moving Average) and the SMA (Simple/Smoothed Moving Average) are compared below.

7.2.2.1 Differences between the EMA and the SMA

EMA and SMA differ only in the calculation of the average price. The EMA gives more weight to the last candlesticks and therefore moves faster than the SMA. The SMA weights all candlesticks equally over the observation period. The comparison in figure 65 clearly shows that the EMA adapts more quickly to the current price. But is this a good thing or a bad thing?

7.2.2.2 Advantages and disadvantages – EMA vs. SMA

The answer is neither. The advantages of one MA are the disadvantages of the other and vice versa.

Figure 65 shows that the **EMA** reacts **faster** when the price changes direction. However, this also means that the EMA is more susceptible to giving signals too early, and there are more noise signals. On the other hand, the **SMA** adapts more **slowly** to current price movements and can thus filter out noise in a better manner. However, traders using the SMA will also notice changes in direction later since the signals are displayed more slowly.

Ultimately, there is no right or wrong here, which is often the case in trading. It primarily depends on the preferences of a trader and how he/she integrates the MA into his/her trading.

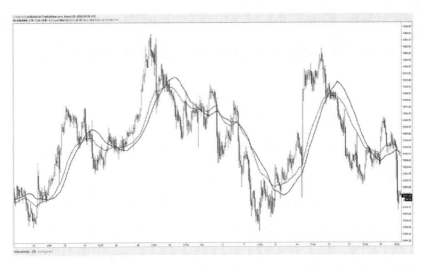

Figure 65: *The EMA reacts significantly faster than the SMA when prices rise and fall.*

7.2.3 What is the best setting for an MA?

The next question that arises about the MA is that of the best time setting and period selection. We need to consider a few aspects for this:

7.2.3.1 Swing trading- vs. day trading

The time horizon and the style of your own trading are decisive for selecting the right MA. Those, who like to hold trades over a longer time period and do not want to be pushed out of the market due to initial smaller correction movements should choose a higher number of periods for their MA. However, those, who tend to react quickly to price fluctuations and want to enter and exit the market immediately, are better off with a shorter number of periods.

A distinction is also made between **day traders**, who usually trade within time frames of 30 minutes and smaller, and **swing traders**, who can be found in the 1H, the 4H or the one-day time frames.

Day traders must react quickly to price changes and have many trades per day. For swing traders, long-term and strategic thinking is important since they often hold their trades for days.

The following guidelines apply for selecting the number of periods of an MA:

- **9 or 10 periods**: These settings are popular because the MAs react quickly to price changes. This number of periods is particularly suitable for day trading in lower time frames.

- **20/21 periods**: This is the range of medium-term MAs that can be used in smaller as well as higher time frames. The 21-period MA is a universal tool.

- **50 periods**: The 50-period MA is very popular. It is often used as a support and resistance tool, since it is generally well respected by the price – keyword: self-fulfilling prophecy. The 50-period MA is used as a trend tool by long-term traders, because it analyses a longer time frame.

- **100 and 200 periods**: These MAs are regularly used by swing traders in the high time frames. On television and in the financial media, you can often also see that the analysts fall back on the 100- or 200-period MA. These MAs are also repeatedly used as support and resistance as figure 66 shows.

Figure 66: The 100- and 200-period MAs effectively describe trend phases and trend direction. Support and resistance also act as support and resistance as indicated by the Xs.

7.2.3.2 Self-fulfilling prophecy

I advise sticking to commonly used MAs, because the factor of self-fulfilling prophecy should not be underestimated in this case either. When millions of traders, the financial media and even algorithms (programs that make automatic buy and sell decisions) use the same MAs, they strengthen the impact of these MAs.

7.2.4 How to use MAs – the five signals

If we now look at trading using an MA, we can distinguish between five types of signals:

7.2.4.1 Trend direction and filter

The legendary trader Marty Schwartz was featured in the book "Market Wizards". He is a staunch supporter of MAs. In his own book, "Pit Bull: Lessons from Wall Street's Champion Day Trader", he says the following about the use of MAs:

"The 10-day EMA is my favourite indicator to determine the trend. I call it 'red light, green light' because trading requires you to trade on the right side of the MA to maximise the probability of profits. If the price is above the 10-day EMA, you have the green light. The market will be in a positive mood and you should think about buying. On the other hand, a price below the 10-EMA indicates a red light. The market is in a negative mood and you should think about selling."

Thus, Marty Schwartz uses his MA to determine the trend direction and to distinguish between buy and sell signals. This is a good tip, because you should never buy when the price is in an overall downward trend – and an MA acts as a filter.

The following rule is applicable for such a trading strategy: If the price is above the MA, you should search for buy trades, and search for sell trades if the price is below the MA. This way traders can go with the higher-level trend which usually results in smoother trading opportunities.

Determining the higher-level trend in a higher time frame using an MA and then planning the entries in this direction in the lower time frame has proven to be particularly effective. Figure 67 shows how the 100 period MA described the long-term trend direction effectively.

Figure 67: The long-term 100-period MA acts as a trend direction filter if the price is in a trend phase. When the price is above the MA, the market is in an upward trend and vice versa. A break of the MA is an important signal.

7.2.4.2 Golden cross trading strategy

The golden cross is a popular trend following system. A golden cross is formed when the 50-period and 200-period MAs cross. The underlying idea is: if the short-term MA falls below the long-term MA, this indicates an important turnaround since the current prices fall below the long-term average.

As indicated by the golden crosses shown in figure 68, this signal is often suitable for determining the long-term trend and identifying changes in the trend direction. The vertical lines mark the cross-over signals.

It does not necessarily have to be the 50-period and 200-period MAs. Another popular combination is the 12-period and 26-period MAs. It reacts faster due to the smaller number of periods and is usually better suited for short-term traders.

Figure 68: The Golden Cross signal can often indicate the start of a new trend phase. In this case, the 50-period and 100-period MAs were used in a 4-hour chart. MAs are universally applicable.

7.2.4.3 Support and resistance (S&R)

As already mentioned, MAs are so important because they are used by a lot of traders. For this reason, MAs can also be used ideally as an S&R tool. It is important only to stick to the most popular period settings to make use of this effect.

In an upward trend, many traders use the MA to find re-entries in the prevailing trend direction when the price moves back into the MA range during a correction. This is also known as **pullback trading**. If the price is supported at an MA, this represents a buy signal for many traders.

Especially the long-term MAs like the 50-period, 100-period or 200-period MAs are effective tools in this context, because several traders use them – keyword: self-fulfilling prophecy.

Figure 69 marks each support and resistance contact point at the MAs with an X. As with trend lines, traders often use those contact points to find trend trading opportunities into the overall trend direction.

Figure 69: This chart analysis uses a 200 period MA. The price respects it as support and resistance at almost every contact point. If you now add other concepts such as highs and lows, you can clearly explain the price developments in a proper manner.

7.2.4.4 Distance from the MA

The distance between the price and the MA indicates the strength of a trend. The farther the price can move away from the MA, the stronger the movement. If the price approaches the MA

133

again or even breaks it, this can be an important trend reversal signal.

If the distance between the price and the MA increases, this may indicate that a trend is no longer sustainable. An explosive leap away from the MA should always be a warning to be extremely careful and wait for trend reversal signals – similar to the bump-and-run formation.

Figure 70 demonstrates that the price moves away from the MA during strong trend phases. When the price then breaks the MA, as indicated by the vertical lines, a shift in trend direction can often be the result.

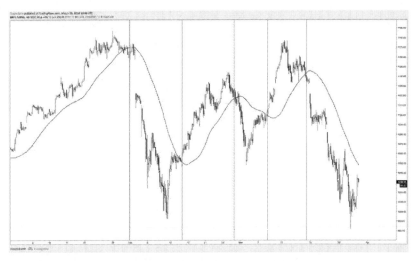

Figure 70: This chart analysis uses a 50-period MA and shows its effectiveness in a comprehensible manner. During trend phases, the price moves away from its MA. When a trend comes to an end, the price first approaches the MA and then breaches it completely. The horizontal lines mark these breaches and it is always the starting point of a prolonged trend phase.

7.2.4.5 Momentum

The distance between two MAs provides information about the momentum: The further the two MAs move apart, the stronger the prevailing trend. A short-term and a long-term MA are normally used for this type of price analysis. For example, traders can use the 12-period and 26-period MAs, which are also the basis of the MACD indicator that we will discuss in the next section.

There are two possible signals and applications: The trader waits for the two MAs to cross and separate, indicating the start of a trend. As long as the MAs do not cross or converge, the prevailing trend is still intact. A trend reversal is initiated when both the MAs converge and eventually cross. The vertical lines in figure 71 mark the crosses of the two MAs. A cross often indicates a change in trend direction effectively.

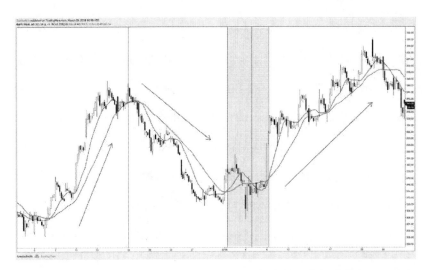

Figure 71: If the two MAs intersect, a new trend is initiated. During the trend phases, the distance between the two MAs indicates the strength of a trend. In the shaded area, the MA has displayed false signals because the price has moved sideways. One 12-period and one 26-period MAs were used.

7.3 RSI indicator

The RSI indicator is one of the most popular indicators among traders because it is versatile and often provides good signals when used in the right situations.

The RSI is a momentum indicator: it indicates the direction and strength of a price movement.

7.3.1 Introduction: Understanding the RSI

The default setting of the RSI uses 14 periods, i.e. the RSI analyses and compares the last 14 candlesticks.

The RSI compares the **average profit** and **average loss**. It analyses how many of the last 14 candlesticks have risen and how many have fallen and also compares their sizes.

The values of the RSI range between 0 and 100, which makes it an oscillator.

For example, if **all** 14 past candlesticks have risen, then the RSI would indicate a value of 100. If all the last 14 candlesticks have fallen, the RSI would indicate a value of 0. If we consider a scenario in which half of the candlesticks have risen and the other half has fallen and the candlesticks have nearly the same size, the RSI would show a value of 50. The more the candlesticks have risen and the larger their size, the higher the RSI. This is still very superficial and we will now carry out more detailed chart analyses.

7.3.2 Chart example 1

The framed area in figure 72 shows an upward trend over 14 candlesticks; all these candlesticks, except two, are rising candlesticks. In addition, the rising candlesticks are mostly relatively large and without pronounced candlestick shadows. As a result, the RSI shows a high value at 75, confirming the upward trend with a lot of momentum.

Figure 72: The RSI indicator analyses the direction and size of the last 14 candlesticks and indicates the strength of the current price movement.

7.3.3 Chart example 2

Three different areas are marked in figure 73.

We can see a strong downward trend in the first area, during which almost all candlesticks, except a few small Doji candlesticks, have fallen. As a result, the RSI has fallen to 17, confirming a strong downward trend.

The middle area shows a relatively strong upward trend: The RSI has reached the level of 70, and the falling candlesticks are also usually much smaller. This is an indication that the buyers have majority.

The third area shows a sideways movement over 14 candlesticks. The RSI is 42, which means there is no trend. Although the price falls slightly, which is confirmed by the value that is less than 50, the strength ratio is rather balanced.

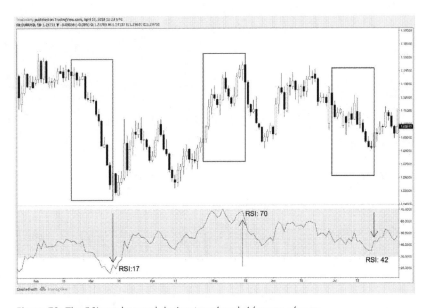

Figure 73: The RSI can be used during trend and sideways phases.

If you would take the time to look closely at the last 14 candlesticks and analyse them, you could often omit the RSI.

However, an indicator is always a good tool to shorten the analysis time and to get objective confirmation.

7.3.4 The myth of oversold and overbought

We will now discuss the biggest misunderstanding as far as indicators are concerned. The terms **overbought** and **oversold** are used when the RSI indicates values above 70 or below 30. With these terms, traders mistakenly believe that the trend is now more likely to reverse.

However, this is completely wrong because, as we have seen, a high RSI confirms a strong upward trend and a low RSI indicates a strong downward trend. At extreme values, the RSI does **not** indicate that the trend is weakening or will soon be over, but rather confirms that this is a period of high momentum. A trader, who is now constantly trying to sell during a strong upward trend, will soon get into trouble.

Figure 74 shows such an example. In the first marked area, the RSI entered the overbought region above 70 for the first time. As you can see, the upward trend continued for a very long time and even after it had initially flattened out, there was no trend reversal. Instead, the price has again reached the overbought status in the second marked area and continued its upward trend. Naturally, a high RSI only means that the upward trend is very strong and dominated by the buyers, and not that it will lead to a trend reversal.

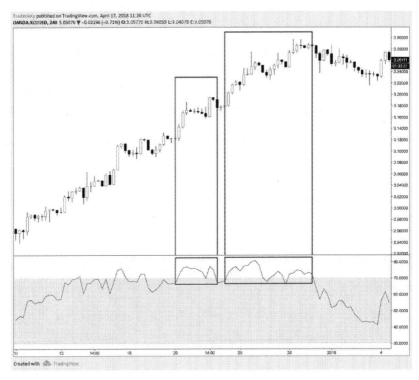

Figure 74: Overbought and oversold are not signals indicating that the prevailing trend will soon reverse, but that the trend is developing very strongly in one direction.

7.3.5 RSI for support and resistance

Since the RSI is effective in analysing the momentum and strength of a price movement, it can also be used efficiently for support and resistance trading.

In the example given in figure 75, the horizontal line indicates a strong resistance level in the DAX, which the price has repeatedly

142

tested. In the first two contact attempts, the RSI shows values of 55 and 61, which means that there were more buyers than sellers in the market, but the buyers did not have the absolute majority.

At the third contact point, the RSI has a value of 68, which indicates a stronger movement. Although the price did not manage to break the resistance at this point, it returned to this point relatively quickly. As shown in an earlier chapter, such a quick return to a price level confirms that buyers are gaining strength. In the final breakout attempt, the RSI reached a value of 74. It can be clearly seen the bullish candlesticks are prevalent, which ultimately led to the breakout. The breakout has been accompanied by a price jump, which is also a strong signal to buy. It is important to emphasise that the final breakout signal was generated only when the price closed above the resistance.

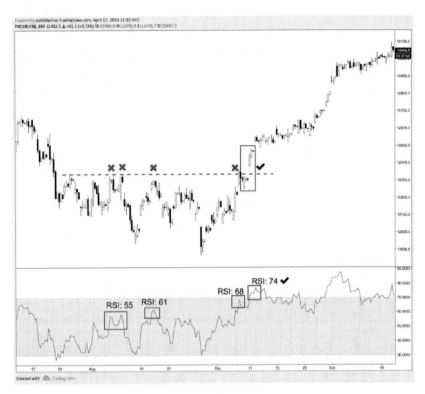

Figure 75: The RSI can also be used for breakout trading. A breakout with a high RSI value has a better chance of success.

7.3.6 RSI divergence

The divergence is my favourite signal when it comes to the RSI. Unlike the overbought and oversold signals, it can often indicate a real trend reversal precisely.

The divergence shows a signal wherein the price and the indicator do not match (diverge). A divergence occurs when the price reaches a new high during an uptrend trend, but the RSI creates a lower high.

The left scenario in figure 76 shows the classic divergence when the price made higher highs, but the RSI divergence indicates that the final uptrend wave was already less strong.

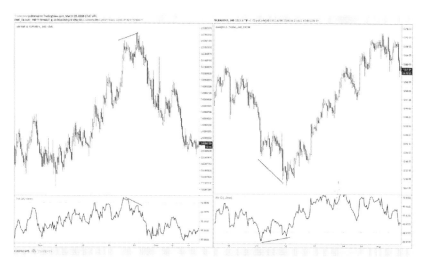

Figure 76: RSI divergences may indicate a change in the trend direction in advance as they indicate decreasing momentum.

An RSI divergence, therefore, exists when the trend appears to have continued on the price chart, but the RSI already indicates that something has changed in the ratio between the buyers and the sellers, and the last trend wave was not as strong.

Figure 77 shows another example: At the end of the downward trend, the RSI has formed a divergence and indicated the subsequent trend reversal in advance. Although the price formed a lower low, the last downward trend wave was significantly shorter and, thus, weaker. The price has barely managed to reach a new low. This decreasing trend strength was confirmed by the RSI divergence. Our knowledge of price waves now complements the RSI analysis. We can clearly see how price waves truly are the building blocks of all trend and chart analyses.

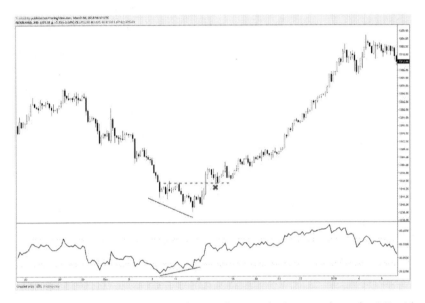

Figure 77: Although the last trend wave has reached a new low, the RSI with divergence shows that this last trend wave has lost its strength. Therefore, we can see an additional retest.

7.4 Stochastic indicator

The Stochastic indicator provides information about the momentum and the trend strength; it shows how **quickly** and how **strongly** the price moves.

The developer of the Stochastic, Georg Lane, says:

"Stochastics measures the momentum of price. If you visualize a rocket going up in the air – before it can turn down, it must slow down. Momentum always changes direction before price."

George Lane[7], developer of the Stochastic indicator

The price does not change the direction suddenly. A prevailing trend first slows down and then changes direction step by step. We have often seen this behaviour in our previous wave analysis as well.

7.4.1 How does the Stochastic momentum measure?

The default settings of the Stochastic indicator are usually set to either 14 or 5 periods. In our examples, we will limit ourselves to the 5-period setting. However, the usage is identical for 14 periods.

---

[7] George Lane (technical analyst):
http://en.wikipedia.org/wiki/George_Lane_%28technical_analyst%29

The Stochastic indicator analyses the absolute high and the absolute low and compares them with the closing price of the selected period.

Example 1: A high Stochastic

A high Stochastic means that the price has closed near the absolute high of past five candlesticks.

In figure 78, the high across the last five candlesticks is $100, the low is $60, and the price closed at $95. The Stochastic gives us a value of 88 (88%). This means that the price closed only 12% (100% minus 88%) below the absolute high of this period.

With this knowledge, we can already understand the Stochastic in a much better manner: A high Stochastic means that the price has closed near the absolute high and that the buyers control the proceedings at present.

Calculation:

Absolute low across five candlesticks: $60

High across five candlesticks: $100

Closing price: $95

Calculation: $[(95 - 60)/(100 - 60)]*100 = 88\%$

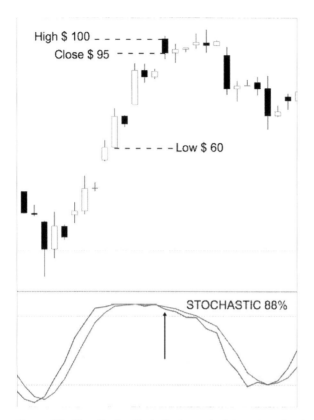

High $ 100
Close $ 95

Low $ 60

STOCHASTIC 88%

Figure 78: The Stochastic indicator calculates strongly the price pushes in the prevailing trend direction and how close the price is to the upper or lower end of the current trend.

Example 2: A low Stochastic

Conversely, a low Stochastic means that the price has closed near the lower end of the period of the last five candlesticks. In figure 79, we can see a Stochastic value of 17%. The Stochastic shows that the price has just closed near its absolute low.

Calculation:

Low price across five candlesticks: $50

High across five candlesticks: $80

Closing price: $55

Calculation: [(55 − 50)/(80 − 50)]*100 = 17%

Figure 79: In this chart example, the Stochastic with a value of 17 indicates that the price has closed near the lower end of the downward trend.

7.4.2 Overbought vs. Oversold

The pitfalls in the interpretation of overbought and oversold must be pointed out once again in connection with the Stochastic.

Traders talk of overbought when the Stochastic value is above 80 and oversold when the Stochastic value falls below 20. But it would be wrong to assume that the price now has a greater chance of reversing.

As we have seen, a low Stochastic only means that the price moves lower strongly. Figure 80 shows that a strong trend is always accompanied by a Stochastic that is in the overbought/oversold range. **Knowing this, overbought does not mean that the trend is likely to reverse, but that the price is in a strong trend.** Traders, who try to sell during a strong trend just because the Stochastic is in the overbought range, will quickly lose their money due to wrong trading decisions and a completely wrong understanding of their trading tools. Trends can remain in the overbought range for a very long time.

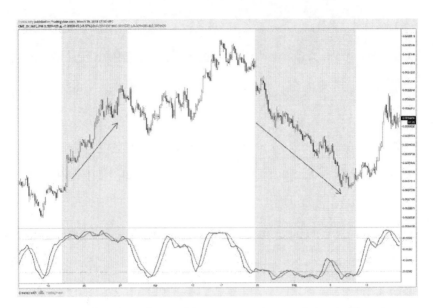

Figure 80: Overbought and oversold are not trend reversal signals. The price may continue to rise or fall for a long time since a high or a low Stochastic signals a strong trend.

7.4.3 The Stochastic signals

The following tips will help you in interpreting the Stochastic quickly and efficiently.

- **Breakout trading:** If the Stochastic suddenly rises sharply, as shown in figure 81, while both Stochastic bands separate, this can often indicate the start of a new trend. The signal shows that the upward trend is gaining momentum and the price is pushed to the high points of the past 14 candlesticks. If this is accompanied by a breakout from a sideways phase, it reinforces the signal.

152

As shown in figure 81, you can also draw trend lines on your indicator and wait for a confirmed breakout as a trading signal.

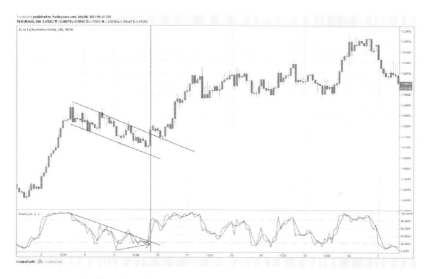

Figure 81: The breakout from the consolidation phase is accompanied by a Stochastic breakout and confirms the rising momentum.

- **Trend-following trading**: As long as the Stochastic continues in one direction, the trend continues. It is not worth fighting the Stochastic. It is better to use the information to remain in the trade with self-confidence.
- **Strong trends:** If the Stochastic is in the oversold and overbought range, you should also remain in the trade, since a very strong trend can be assumed. As we have seen, even if the Stochastic is in the overbought range, it

does not suggest that the trend may tip over — quite the contrary.

Some of my personal trading strategies even use the overbought/oversold characteristic as an entry signal. A new trade is initiated when the STOCHASTIC crosses into overbought or oversold. Figure 82 shows how long trending phases can last while the STOCHASTIC is at its extremes.

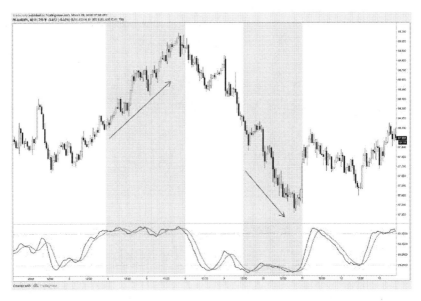

Figure 82: *Even if a trend is eventually reversed after the overbought and oversold scenarios, the price has first continued to rise and fall for a long time. Traders should never trade in case of a trend reversal only based on overbought and oversold signals. Instead, the trend-following trading is the correct approach in such a case.*

- **Divergences**: Like any other momentum indicator, the divergences of the Stochastic can be important signals for identifying possible trend reversal scenarios. If the price and the Stochastic show opposite signals, this represents a divergence. Figure 83 shows the following scenario: Although the price has set a lower low on the left, the Stochastic already indicates that the downward trend strength is declining by printing a higher low. Traders are, thus, warned to enter new sell trades or keep an eye on their existing sell trades and wait for signals to close them in time.

  Trend reversal traders wait until the price reaches a new high and gives them an entry signal.

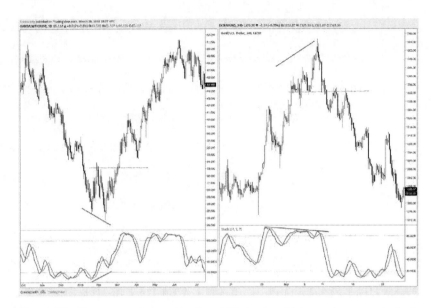

Figure 83: *Divergences in combination with broken highs or lows can indicate effective trend reversal signals.*

7.5 Bollinger Bands®

Bollinger Bands® are versatile and we can use these indicators in numerous situations to complement our trading decisions. Bollinger Bands® are dynamic: They constantly adapt to changing market conditions, which can be a big advantage.

7.5.1 Introduction: Bollinger Bands®

As shown in figure 84, Bollinger Bands® consist of a channel, which encloses the price on both sides, and the middle band which is a moving average (MA).

The outer bands measure the volatility and the extent to which the price fluctuates. The outer bands widen when volatility increases, i.e. when the price moves up and down more strongly, and they contract when the price moves up and down only slightly. The default setting for the channel uses 2.0 standard deviations, but in my trading I prefer to use 2.5 standard deviations, which makes the channel wider and, thus, filter out noise signals more effectively. For the MA in the middle band, I use a 20-period MA, which corresponds to the default settings and is a good compromise for medium-term day and swing traders.

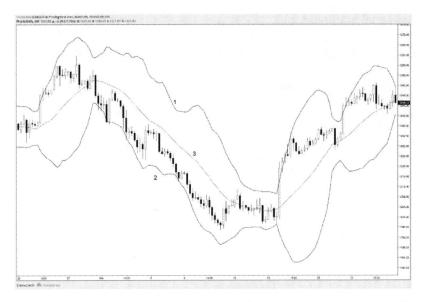

Figure 84: *Points 1 and 2 are the outer Bollinger® bands and the band in the middle (3) is a 20-period MA.*

7.5.2 Trend-following trading using Bollinger Bands®

Bollinger Bands® are made for trend-following trading. Pay attention to the following points in order to use Bollinger Bands® successfully in the trade-following trading:

- During trend phases, the price usually progresses along the **outer** bands. Strong trends are indicated by extended price movements near the outer bands.
- If the price **pulls away** from the outer bands and moves to the **middle**, this can often represent a weakening trend.
- If the price then **breaks** the middle band, it usually signals the end of a trend.

The trend-following properties of Bollinger Bands® can be understood more precisely using the chart analyses in figure 85 and the five points marked in it.

1) The price shows a strong downward trend and progresses **along the outer bands**. Although there are isolated rejection candles with long shadows, the price never leaves the outer bands.

2) The price tries to push down with another trend wave, but does not manage to reach the outer bands – this is an **exhaustion signal**. Trend reversal takes place shortly thereafter: the rising candlesticks become stronger. Your RSI indicator would also confirm a divergence here because the trend waves become shorter.

3) Three declining highs all miss the outer band. This indicates that the upward trend does not have enough buying interest and that the buyers are not able to keep the price up, let alone initiate a break out higher.

4) During another strong downward movement, the price progresses at the outer band, confirming that the sellers clearly dominate the proceedings in the market.

5) Finally, the price cannot reach the outer band. This results in the **trend reversal**.

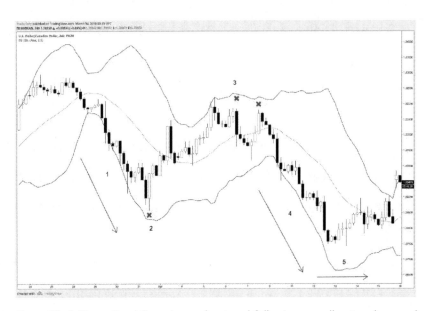

Figure 85: *Bollinger Bands® can be used as trend-following as well as trend reversal signals.*

7.5.3 How to find reversals

For the statistical point of view, the setting of 2.5 standard deviations means that 99% of all price movements take place within the two Bollinger Bands®. Thus, when you see a price movement that breaks the outer bands, it indicates a rare condition. However, we must distinguish between two different situations in such a case:

1) If the price shoots through the outer band and also **closes outside** the outer band. This indicates an extremely strong trend and a continuation is likely.

2) If the price shoots through the outer band and then immediately **reverses**, it indicates rejection.

The chart analysis in figure 86 helps in interpreting this important signal. During the left downward trend phase (1), although the price breaks the outer band several times, it never leads to a complete upward rejection and the price always remains close to the outer bands. At point 2, the price can no longer reach the outer bands and, at point 3, we see the last rising up together with a last weak break-out attempt. At point 4, the price breaks through a past high for the first time and thus signals the start of an upward trend. Near point 5, the price is always close to the outer bands, which confirms an extremely strong upward trend.

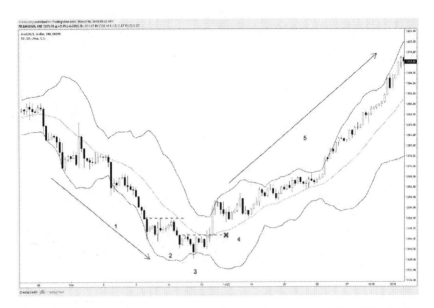

Figure 86: A breach of outer bands can show a strong reversal signal if it is also accompanied by momentum.

7.6 The MACD indicator — Moving Average Convergence Divergence

The MACD is a well-known and popular momentum and trend indicator based on moving averages.

7.6.1 Components of the MACD

Figure 87 shows the MACD has three important components: two lines and one histogram.

MACD line: The MACD line is the heart of the MACD. It represents the difference between the 12-period and 26-period EMA (EMA = exponential moving average). The MACD is essentially a complete MA crossover system. Crossover systems are very popular because they can effectively determine the trend direction, trend strength and trend changes through MA analysis.

Signal line: The signal line is the 9-period EMA of the MACD line.

MACD histogram: The histogram in the MACD is the difference between the signal line and the MACD line.

In this section, we focus on the MACD and signal lines, since the two lines can give meaningful signals collectively. The histogram is not a deciding factor for our purposes, because it does not improve the signal strength significantly.

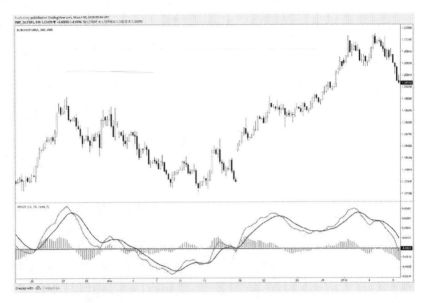

Figure 87: Standard display of the MACD indicator with the histogram in the background, which is not required for our analysis purposes. The faster reacting line is the MACD line and the slower progressing line is the signal line. We use the default settings of 12, 26 and 9 periods.

7.6.2 Two trading signals of the MACD

When it comes to using the MACD, two trading strategies are particularly effective:

7.6.2.1 The MACD lines 0-level crossover

The vertical lines in figure 88 mark the points at which the MACD line crosses the 0-level. The 26-period and the 12-period

MAs are shown for clarity right on the price chart. A crossing of averages on the charts provides the identical signals to that of the MACD lines, because the MACD uses these two averages as described above.

When two moving averages cross, this signals a change in the trend structure. If a short MA crosses the long-term MA downwards, this means that current prices have fallen below the long-term average. This often indicates a new downward trend. The horizontal lines mark the MA crossovers.

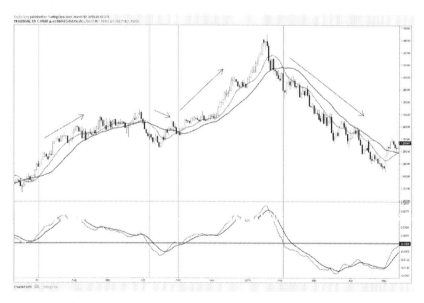

Figure 88: If the two MAs intersect, this is also the sign that the MACD is giving a new signal. This chart analysis clearly shows that the MACD lines can effectively indicate a trend change and confirm the trend direction.

7.6.2.2 Signal line

In the MACD window, when we see that the two lines separate, it means that the trend is gaining strength because the current prices are rising faster than the past prices. The further the two lines move apart, the stronger the trend is. When the two lines converge, this indicates a slowdown in the trend.

As long as the price is running above the moving averages and the MACD lines are also above 0, we are in an upward trend. This often helps in understanding the price in a better manner.

Figure 89 shows how well the Signal lines can indicate the trend direction. The vertical lines mark the crossovers.

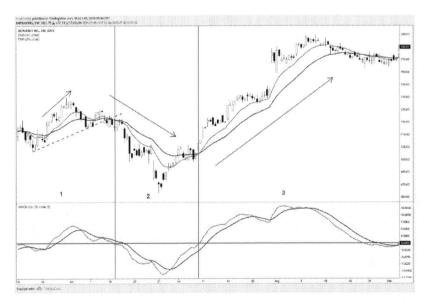

Figure 89: The section at point 1 shows a short upward trend. Both MACD lines quickly cross again. In section 2, we can see a slightly stronger trend; both MACD lines

During sideways markets, the MACD and signal lines are very close to each other and fluctuate around the 0-level, which means that there is no momentum and no trend. Just like the MA, the MACD should not be used during sideways phases.

If the price then suddenly breaks out and moves in one direction, both MACD lines will also separate and begin to rise. Many traders also use horizontal support and resistance lines in their MACD to identify such breakouts.

When the MACD and signal lines flatten again and reach the 0-level, the trend is over. Naturally, this does not immediately mean that the price changes the direction completely, but only that the trend is losing strength.

7.6.3 Use of MACD signals

Figure 90 shows a classic example of how the MACD can be used for trading signals. After the price breaks the trend line on the left on MACD (1), it has started a new upward trend (2). During the trend, the MACD line has always been above 0 and the price has, therefore, also risen steadily above the MAs (2).

During the consolidation phase (3), we can use trend lines to identify a wedge. If the price breaks out of this, the MACD also starts to rise and separate again (4).

At the end of the trend, we can spot a divergence (5). A trend reversal is very likely now, because the divergence signals decreasing buying interest. The subsequent break by the MAs is also accompanied by a fall of the MACD line below the 0-level and initiates the new downward trend (6).

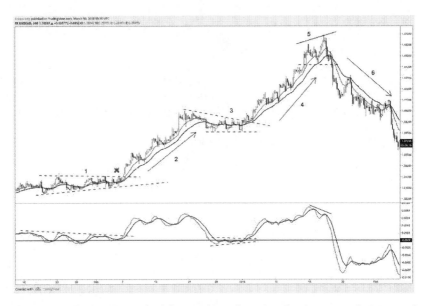

Figure 90: The MACD is ideal for tracking the price developments during trend markets.

7.6.4 MACD divergence

In the chart shown in figure 91, although the price formed new highs during the upward trend, the MACD was able to form lower highs and thus a divergence.

Now a trader has to wait until the price actively breaks through the MAs and, in the most favourable case, also reaches a new low on the charts.

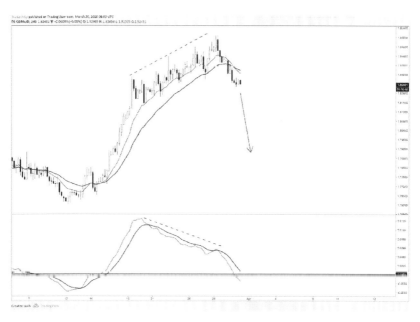

Figure 91: The MACD divergence signals the trend direction reversal in advance.

7.7 What is the best indicator?

At the end of this chapter on indicators, let me make it very clear once again: **no indicator is better than the other!** It always depends on the area of application and the usage by the trader. An indicator is a tool developed for a specific purpose. Most traders make the mistake of using their indicators during inappropriate market conditions.

For example, a hammer is only useful for hitting the nail; it fails if you try to use it for tightening the screws. However, it cannot be generalised that a hammer is not a suitable tool. It is just that it is not useful for all purposes.

The same applies to the indicators. First, the market conditions must be clear: Are we in a trend phase or a sideways phase? An appropriate indicator can then be selected to carry out an effective analysis.

Moreover, an indicator, as the name implies, does not provide independent signals, but only certain indications. It supports the decision-making process, but should not justify it. Indicators should therefore only be used to obtain further confluence signals.

I put together a free webinar at www.tradeciety.com/indicators to further illustrate how to understand, combine and use indicators on your charts.

8. Your journey as a trader

This book brings together a lot of knowledge and even more practical tips and food for thought for your own trading. From my own experience I know that, despite intensive reading and lots of aha-moments, the application is not at all easy, and doubts and fears quickly gain the upper hand.

In order to help you make the next step in your trading journey, and to provide you with even more practical and ready-to-use trading strategies, I have prepared a final website with a 10-step process for all readers.

To further strengthen your knowledge about technical analysis and to challenge your understanding, visit www.tradeciety.com/next in order to complete the final step.

Made in the USA
Columbia, SC
17 September 2020

20955489R10100